Country, Cookin'

Compiled by:
Rozell Fair Fabiani
and
Callaway Gardens

1980

Additional copies of Country Cookin'
are available by writing or calling
The Gardens Country Store, Pine Mountain,
Georgia 31822 (404)663-2281.

Published and Printed by
The Marketing Department of Callaway Gardens

Typeset by Shirley Harrington

FOREWORD

This cookbook is dedicated to the past and is in response to the many requests we have received for recipes of the South and from our own kitchens. You'll also find recipes from all over the world reflecting the South's favor as a place for international visitors and investment.

Years before it became fashionable, rural cooking was the only kind of cooking known to the people of this area. And when the resort operation expanded to accommodate the many visitors to the grand experiment of Cason J. Callaway, Sr. called Callaway Gardens, it was only natural the local cooks who worked in the kitchens continue to cook the foods in the style native to this area. Yet, "Country Cookin'" is more than recipes. It is about the role of food in the homes of the South: a medium for gathering, for sharing and for enjoying the bounty of the land and the people who work it.

The recipes in this book were collected and tested by Rozell Fabiani, this area's longest running TV personality on WRBL-TV from Columbus, Georgia. For nearly thirty years, area residents have enjoyed her show and the cooking features presented by Home Economists, international visitors to Fort Benning, and nationally famous chefs. There is always something good cooking on Rozell's show every day.

To the memory of the rural southern table and its importance in shaping our lives and to Rozell Fabiani, this book is dedicated.

COUNTRY COOKIN'
from
Callaway Gardens

When you think of country living, you think of "the good things in life"....the simple life....filled with simple pleasures....good fresh air and plenty of good country food....fresh vegetables, fresh fruits, fresh eggs and milk and meats from the farm....cracklin' good!

When you think of Callaway Gardens....you think of the good things in life! Plenty of fresh air....acres and acres of spring pure lakes....miles and miles of beautiful trees beside paths made for walking....and thousands of plants and flowers....yours for enjoying!

There's a Chapel beside a lake....with waterfalls rippling over rocks and a stone bench....yours for meditation....just outside the Chapel! Inside the Chapel, dedicated to Mr. Cason Callaway's mother, Ida Cason Callaway, a stone altar....windows created from hand stained glass to reflect the four seasons of Callaway Gardens....and ever so often on a holiday or the weekend....you hear the golden chimes of the organ in the Chapel....ringing out across the countryside....reminding folks with joyous hymns and songs of praise....that God still rules the universe and this place is dedicated to His glory!

There are golf courses....where folks can "get away from it all" and enjoy golf at its best....courses surrounded with all the beauty Nature can afford....which makes the playing better even when you're playing bad!

There are walks and trails to be enjoyed every day of the year. . . . chrysanthemum trails. . . . holly berry trails. . . . a trail where the jonquils grow. . . . and down by the lakes. . . . mountain laurel and rhododendron. . . . crepe myrtles and roses. . . . wild flowers galore! There's just so much of natural beauty in this country side garden. . . . you just want to give thanks for the folks who make it all possible for you to enjoy!

There's a country cabin. . . . where you get an authentic glimpse into yesterday and how it was for folks 'way back when. . . . its a lesson in history that you don't want to miss. . . .

And then. . . . there's Mr. Cason's Vegetable Garden. . . . and Oh. . . . the fragrance of the herbs. . . . the beauty of row after row of squash and pumpkin. . . . corn and beans. . . . tomatoes and potatoes. . . . peppers and peas. . . . on and on. . . . a country gardens at its best. . . . for that's what Mr. Cason intended it to be. . . . where things grow so folks can see how God, Nature and man work together to feed the world. . . .

There's a man made beach where folks can play and while away the time in the summer sun. . . . a lake to swim in. . . . and lakes to fish in. . . boats for riding in. . . . and skiing on. . . .

And "up the road a piece". . . . there's the Country Store! Reminiscent of the country stores of yesterday. . . . but filled with all the exotic, good things of today as well. . . . Country hams and caviar. . . . pickles, jams and jellies. . . . candies and nuts. . . . and "the food of gods and the gardens. . . . "Muscadines! Muscadine jelly. . . . Muscadine preserves and sauce!. . . . Packaged for gifts to be sent anywhere in the world! Gifts of all kinds at the Country Store. . . . and if you're a bit hungry. . . . try some of the Country Store's "feed bags". . . . or just a country ham sandwich! Country eatin' is at its best here!

And then. . . . the Inn at Callaway Gardens. . . . tucked away against Pine Mountain. . . . looking out across the golf courses to the lakes and trees. . . . You can be alone if you like or join the many other people who come to the Inn for meetings for conventions or just for a "taste of the good life"! In the dining room you'll get a taste of just how good food can be. . . . all those garden grown vegetables. . . . country ham and turkey. . . . chicken and seafood. . . . and all the trimmings. . . . topped off with pecan pie. . . . the best apple crumb pie you ever ate. . . . and the dessert that tops them all. . . . Callaway Garden's Muscadine ice cream!

Now. . . . if all this is not enough to "whet" your appetite for good country livin and eatin. . . . don't know what would! And so that you can take a taste of it home with you. . . . we've compiled this cookbook for your enjoyment. You'll find some of the Gardens favorite recipes along with hundreds of others which compliment the purpose of recipes you can make from the cupboard, the ice box, or from the garden!

One more thing. . . . when you come to the Gardens. . . . take the time to stop at the Information Center first. . . . in just a few minutes you'll understand the purpose in the planning of this "garden spot" of the world. . . . and you'll get and insight into the beauty of the mind and the soul of the people who had a dream and made it come true for all of us. Generation after generation, ... to enjoy. . . . Cason and Virginia Callaway!

Happy lookin' and Happy cookin'
with COUNTRY COOKIN'
from CALLAWAY GARDENS

COUNTRY COOKIN'
from CALLAWAY GARDENS

To Whet the Appetite

TO WHET THE APPETITE

To Whet The Appetite. . . . must look good and taste good. . . . little bits of colorful, tasty canapes' or dips or hors d' oeuvres (French for relish!) should always be served in small portions since the purpose is to whet and not to satisfy the appetite!

Try some of these new ideas with some old fashioned ingredients you'll always find in the pantry!. . . .

HAM PUFFS

Use your favorite pie crust recipe or. . . .something our grandmothers would love to have had on hand. . . .PIECRUST MIX from the grocery shelf!

2 sticks piecrust mix
1⅓ cups boiling hot water
⅛ teaspoon cayenne pepper
⅔ cups chutney, finely chopped
⅔ cups finely chopped celery
4 cups ground cooked ham
¼ cup mayonnaise
4 eggs

Crumble pie crust mix in heavy sauce pan. . . .slowly add boiling water and stir vigorously over low, low heat until pastry forms a ball and leaves sides of pan. Cook for one minute more stirring constantly. Remove from heat, add slightly beaten eggs and beat hard with hand beater or on slow speed of electric mixer for about two minutes. Heat oven to 425°. Drop batter by teaspoons on ungreased sheet.

Filling:
Mix the chopped ham with chopped celery and chutney. . . .add cayenne pepper and mayonnaise. Chill thoroughly before filling puffs.
Serves: 80 puffs

Bake for about 20 - 25 minutes or until golden brown. Cool on rack but keep out of draft (this would make them fall!). Split when cool and remove inside if desired. Fill with ham mixture just before serving. Do not fill ahead of time (this would make them soggy).

From up Williamsburg way comes a recipe using country ham. . . .so stop by the Country Store, pick up a ham, and follow these directions. . . .

COUNTRY HAM STRAWS

2 cups flour
1 level teaspoon baking powder
½ teaspoon salt
½ cup milk
¾ cup ground Country Ham
½ cup butter
¼ teaspoon paprika
⅛ teaspoon crushed red pepper
1 egg

Sift dry ingredients three or four times. Cut in butter, add whole egg without beating and stir. Add milk and ham and mix well. Roll very thin, cut in strips about ¼ inch wide and four inches long and lay in rows in buttered pan about ¾ inch apart. Bake in moderate oven (350°F) until pale brown. Serve with salads, soups, or breakfast coffee.

SPINACH SQUARES

2 (10 oz) packages frozen
   chopped spinach
6 slices bacon
2 tablespoons chopped onion
4 eggs, slightly beaten
1 cup milk
1 teaspoon salt
¼ teaspoon pepper
2 hardcooked eggs, chopped

Cook spinach as directed on package; drain well. Fry bacon until crisp; reserve dripping. Drain bacon on absorbent paper and crumble. Saute onion in 2 tablespoons bacon dripping until tender Combine all ingredients. Pour mixture into a greased, oblong two quart baking dish. Bake at 350°F. for 35 to 40 minutes or until knife inserted in center comes out clean. Cut in small squares. Serve hot.

OPEN SESAME PASTRY CUPS

1 recipe pie crust mix
2-3 tablespoons sesame seeds
2 (3 oz.) packages cream cheese
2 tablespoons minced chives
⅛ teaspoon crushed red pepper
1 4¾ oz. can liverwurst spread
stuffed olives
pitted black olives

Prepare pie crust according to package directions. Add sesame seeds and crushed red pepper to mix. Chill and roll pastry into large rectangle, cut into about 3 dozen (2 inch) rounds. Place each in a small muffin tin and bake at 400°F about 15 minutes until golden brown. Cool and fill as follows: first a layer of cream cheese mixed with minced chives, a second layer of liverwurst spread, then a top layer of plain cream cheese. Garnish with ripe or stuffed olives. Makes about 3 dozen "cups".

SPRIMP MOLD

1 can tomato soup
2 cans cooked peeled shrimp
1 8 oz. package cream cheese
1 tablespoon grated onion
*1 pkg. gelatin dissolved in ¼ cup
   hot water
1 tablespoon Worcestershire sauce
1 garlic bud, crushed

Dissolve gelatin in ¼ cup hot water. Blend cream cheese, grated onion, minced garlic, Worcestershire sauce, and soup. Add gelatin and shrimp. Pour into mold and refrigerate until congealed. This is delicious served with sesame seed crackers.

*By omitting the gelatin, you have a delicious dip!

A finger sandwich....bound to please...you'll like the tangy sweet taste....!

TEA-PARTY PLEASERS

1 4½-oz. can deviled ham
4 teaspoons frozen orange juice
   concentrate
3 oz. pkg. cream cheese, softened
1 teaspoon sugar
¼ teaspoon finely grated lemon

   peel
1 tablespoon finely chopped nuts
1 tablespoon frozen orange juice
   concentrate
3-4 slices white bread

Combine deviled ham and 4 teaspoons orange juice; chill. Combine softened cream cheese, sugar and nuts. Gradually blend in 1 tablespoon orange juice and lemon peel until mixture is smooth.
Trim crusts from bread slices. Cut each slice into 3 "fingers". Using a cookie press, cover each finger with alternate rows of deviled ham mixture and cream cheese mixture. Makes 9-12 "fingers".

OPEN-FACE CHEESE SANDWICHES

Slice tomatoes paper thin.
Marinate tomatoes with:
salt
pepper
garlic salt
onion salt
Italian seasonings
oregano
regular salad oil mixed with olive
   oil to taste

Toast rounds of bread. Put one layer of American cheese (¼ slice) on top and then the marinated tomatoes. Add some grated Parmesan cheese; mushrooms or sausage can be added to taste. Broil in a very hot oven for about 5 minutes or until cheese is bubbly. Serve while hot. MMMM..good!

Use amounts of ingredients above according to the number of sandwiches you wish to make. Suggest starting with one cup of oil and add other ingredients to taste.

Joreka Loomis, from General Electric, says "these are real appetizers...."

CHEESE WAFERS

2 sticks butter, softened
2 cups sharp cheddar cheese,
   grated
2 cups all-purpose flour
2 cups Rice Crispies

1 tablespoon Salad Supreme
   Dressing Mix (McCormick's)
dash Tabasco

Preheat oven to 350°F. Combine all ingredients. Form into workable dough. Roll into four sticks (about 1½ inches in diameter). Chill thoroughly. Slice into ⅛ inch slices.
Bake at 350°F. for 20 minutes. Makes about 6 dozen. Can be wrapped in foil and frozen and baked when desired.

And here's a tasty bite which has been passed from neighbor to neighbor for years. . . . it's a hit!

HOT CHEESE OLIVES

1 large bottle of stuffed olives
1 box pie crust mix
1 cup grated Cheddar cheese
¼ teaspoon crushed red pepper
    (or cayenne)

Mix pie crust mix with crushed red peppers and cheese. Roll thin and cut in squares. Roll olives in dough and bake at 450°F. The olive balls can be made ahead and kept in the freezer before cooking. Serve hot.

A variation of this recipe. . . . Stuff pitted dates with ½ pecan. Roll in cheese pastry and bake. Watch carefully so these will not overcook. . . . should be lightly browned on bottom.

Cheese log for the holidays. . . . or any day! Eleanor Crozier, long time Director of Home Economics for Nabisco, shared this recipe with us many years ago.

HOLIDAY CHEESE LOG

2 3-oz packages cream cheese, softened
6 oz. finely grated sharp Cheddar cheese
6 oz. finely grated Gruyere or Swiss cheese
1 3-oz. package Roquefort cheese, crumbled
⅛ teaspoon cayenne
3 tablespoons finely chopped ripe olives
3 tablespoons white wine
26 Ritz crackers

⅔ cup finely chopped pistachio nuts
Tokay or green grapes, chilled

Blend first five ingredients in small bowl or electric mixer until smooth and light. Stir in next two ingredients. Set aside about one cup. Using ⅔ cup, spread ¼-inch thick on crackers. Put together in stacks of four or five. Stand stacks on edge on wax paper to make log. Spread ⅓ cup over log covering crackers. Roll in nuts. Refrigerate overnight. Chill remainder of spread. Sprinkle pistachio nuts on top. To serve: cut log at 45° angle.
If desired, serve with grapes. Makes 1 (8 to 10-inch) log. Note: log roll may be wrapped in wax paper for easier handling.

ONION CHEESE RIBS

1/3 cup butter
2 cups enriched self-rising flour
   (level cups)
1 tablespoon sugar
1 cup buttermilk
onion salt
Parmesan cheese

Melt butter in 13" x 9½" pan. Stir together flour, sugar. Stir in enough buttermilk to make a soft dough. On floured surface, gently knead dough for 30 seconds or until smooth. Roll dough out on well floured surface to 13" x 9" rectangle. Cut in half lengthwise; then cut into 13 strips crosswise. Dip each strip in pan with melted butter, turning until all sides are buttered. Place strips in rows close together in same pan. Sprinkle ribs with onion salt and Parmesan cheese. Bake in preheated 450°F. oven about 15 minutes or until golden brown. Makes 26 ribs.

Old fashioned tea rooms are almost extinct. . . . but down in Seale, Alabama, "Miss Helen" Joerg still operates one of the last of its kind. . . . Villula Tea Gardens. . . . her tasty green salad is never served without a "round" of her "CHILI CHEESE". . . . and one of the best variations is this:

1 lb. American cheese
½ lb. sharp Cheddar cheese
1 package Philadelphia Cream
   Cheese
1 clove garlic grated
½ tablespoon Worcestershire
   sauce

Grate and mix cheese. Blend thoroughly with the garlic and Worcestershire sauce. Work with hands and form into long roll. Sprinkle chili powder generously on a piece of wax paper. Roll cheese over this several times until thoroughly coated. Chill and slice in thin slices. Serve with salad or on round crackers. Wrap in wax paper to store in refrigerator.

BAKED STUFFED MUSHROOMS

18-20 medium size mushrooms
1 4½-oz. can deviled ham
1 3-oz. package cream cheese
2 tablespoons sour cream
1 tablespoon minced chives
1 egg yolk, lightly beaten
¼ teaspoon Tabasco
¼ teaspoon Worcestershire sauce
¼ cup fine bread crumbs

Clean mushrooms, remove stems and chop. Place mushroom caps, hollow side up, on lightly oiled cookie sheet. Combine deviled ham, cream cheese, sour cream, Tabasco, Worcestershire sauce, chives, and egg yolk; add chopped mushroom stems and fill caps with mixture. Sprinkle top with bread crumbs. Bake at 450°F. For 8-10 minutes. Serve immediately.

MUSHROOM BITES

12 bite size fresh mushrooms
4 tablespoons olive oil
4 tablespoons chopped onion
2 cloves crushed fresh garlic
½ cup bread crumbs
1 teaspoon oregano
1 tablespoon fresh parsley,
    chopped
1 cup finely chopped mushroom
    stems
2 6-oz. cans minced clams and
    juice

Preheat oven to 325°F. Carefully clean mushrooms, reserving all stems. Finely chop stems and combine all ingredients. Stuff into mushrooms and sprinkle with Parmesan cheese. Bake 25 minutes.

This tasty vegetable has become one of the highlights of the hors d'oeuvres tray. . . .

MARINATED MUSHROOMS

⅔ cup olive oil
½ cup mixed herb vinegar
¼ cup lemon juice
½ cup sliced green onions or
    small white onions
1 small clove garlic, fine chopped
¼ cup sugar
½ teaspoon salt
½ teaspoon crushed red peppers
1 lb. large mushrooms, cleaned
    and sliced

Combine all ingredients except mushrooms in large mixing bowl stirring until sugar is dissolved. Toss mushroom slices in this dressing and refrigerate several hours or overnight.
You may want to drain dressing off before serving, but be sure the mushrooms are cold. May be kept in refrigerator several days.

PARTY SAUSAGE BALLS

½ lb. hot pork sausage
2 cups biscuit mix
1 cup sharp Cheddar cheese,
    grated
¼ teaspoon crushed red pepper

Let sausage come to room temperature. Heat oven to 350°F. With hands, combine sausage, cheese and biscuit mix and crushed red peppers. Blend thoroughly. Roll into small balls and place on ungreased baking sheet. Bake 30 minutes. Serve hot. Makes about 60 balls.

PARTY MEATBALLS

1 package (½ lb.) liver sausage
2 eggs, beaten
½ lb. ground beef
1 cup fine dry bread crumbs
¼ cup catsup
¼ teaspoon Tabasco (optional)
½ teaspoon salt
¼ cup butter
1 envelope dry onion soup mix
1½ cups hot water

Combine liver sausage with eggs; add ground beef, bread crumbs, catsup, and salt; mix well. Shape into one-inch balls. Melt butter in skillet; add meatballs and cook until evenly browned, turning carefully. Add soup mix to water. Pour over meatballs. Cover and cook slowly, 15 minutes. Serve with picks. Makes about 4 dozen.

For years. . . . the Home Economists at Nabisco have developed mouth-watering recipes. . . . this is a tasty example. . . .

BEEF SURPRISE BALLS

1 lb. ground beef
1 egg, slightly beaten
¼ cup minced onion
½ teaspoon garlic salt
¼ teaspoon salt
¼ teaspoon ground black pepper
dash of liquid hot pepper
    seasoning (suggest Tabasco)
Enough cheese crackers to make
    1 cup finely rolled crumbs
45 (½-inch) process American
    cheese cubes or small stuffed
    olives

Combine first seven ingredients and ⅔ cup of crumbs. Shape into 45 balls. Press cheese cubes or olives into them. Roll in remaining crumbs. Bake in a preheated moderate oven (375°F.) 15 to 18 minutes or until golden brown. Serve hot with toothpicks. Makes 45 meatballs.

Here's another good appetizer suggestion. . . .

BACON WRAPUPS

Cut bacon strips in half. Wrap around any of the following:
cocktail weiners
cocktail sausage
cooked chicken livers
stuffed green olives
whole mushrooms
water chestnuts
Fasten with pick - broil 5 inches from heat, turning often, until bacon is crisp.

There was usually a pot of cottage cheese "in the making" on the back of the stove in the country kitchen. . . . and there was nothing tastier when made just right! Here are a couple of modern ways for using cottage cheese as an appetizer. . . .

COTTAGE CHEESE BUTTER

4½ oz. cottage cheese
2-3 tablespoons milk
4½ oz. butter or margarine
1 small onion, finely chopped
1 teaspoon finely chopped chives
pinch of salt

Rub the cottage cheese through a seive and add the milk. Cream the butter, then add the finely chopped onion, the chives, and cottage cheese. Season to taste. Spread on toasted bread rounds and garnish with slice of small salad tomato.

ROQUEFORT ROUNDS

4 oz. Roquefort cheese
½ stick pure butter, softened
¼ cup brandy
⅛ teaspoon freshly ground black pepper

Mix all ingredients until well blended. Spread on buttered rounds of your favorite bread. Sprinke with paprika. Bread may be toasted, if desired.

Another quickie spread. . . .

LIVERWURST SPREAD

4 oz. liver sausage
¼ cup sweet butter, softened
¼ cup Cognac
freshly ground black pepper to taste

Mix all ingredients. Spread on toasted rounds of french bread and sprinkle with finely-chopped ripe olives

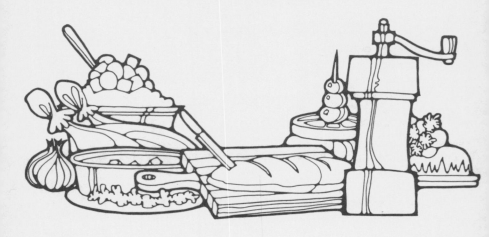

This is a great addition to the Appetizer table. . . .

MUSTARD-MAYONNAISE DIP

1½ cups mayonnaise
4 tablespoons Dijon mustard
Heavy cream (enough to bring mayonnaise to light consistency)
This makes about 2 cups of dip. Use as dip for:
boiled shrimp
sliced cucumbers
radishes
cauliflower
thinly sliced summer squash
celery sticks
green onions
carrot strips
Note: Along with the above, a tray of sliced tomatoes drizzled with a mixture
of salad oil, lemon juice, and McCormick's Salad Supreme, and a little minced parsley. . . . would look mighty pretty and mighty tasty!

Here's a group of dips good for any time of year using sour cream as a base.
Serve with vegetables or your favorite chips. . . .

ROQUEFORT CHEESE DIP

1 cup sour cream
1 thin slice onion
1 teaspoon Worcestershire sauce
3 oz. Roquefort cheese

Cream cheese. Mix with other
ingredients

SHRIMP DIP

1 cup sour cream
1 tablespoon Worcestershire sauce
dash of garlic salt
1 small onion, grated
5 oz. can shrimp, drained
1/2 lb. sharp Cheddar cheese, grated
3 drops of Tabasco

Mix all ingredients until well blended.

BRAUNSCHWEIGER DIP

1/2 lb. Braunschweiger
1 cup sour cream
1 teaspoon Worcestershire sauce
1/2 cup minced bread & butter pickles

Cream all ingredients together.

DEVILED HAM DIP

2 3-oz. pkgs. cream cheese
1 cup sour cream
8 tablespoons deviled ham
2 teaspoons grated onion
1/4 teaspoon salt
1/4 teaspoon pepper

Soften cheese. Mix all ingredients.

HOT COTTAGE CHEESE DIP

1 8-oz. carton cottage cheese
1 cup sharp cheese
1/4 cup white wine
2 tablespoons milk
1 tablespoon finely chopped
    green onion
1/4 teaspoon dry mustard
assorted crackers

In saucepan heat and stir cottage cheese and sharp cheese over low heat until blended. Stir in dry white wine, milk, onion, and dry mustard. Pour into chafing dish. If mixture becomes too thick, you may add a little more milk. Serve with your favorite assorted crackers. Makes 1 2/3 cup.

OLIVE ZIP DIP

2 cups creamed cottage cheese
1/2 cup sour cream
1/2 cup mayonnaise
4 teaspoons prepared horseradish
2 teaspoons grated onion
dash cayenne pepper
dash Tabasco
1 cup finely chopped stuffed olives
assorted fresh vegetables or
    cooked shrimp

Combine cheese, sour cream, mayonnaise, horseradish, onion, cayenne pepper and Tabasco. Blend well. Fold in olives. Serve as a dip for fresh vegetables or cooked shrimp.

From the Meat House and the Creek

FROM THE MEAT HOUSE AND THE CREEK

About meat. . . .

Most of us, when we plan a meal, think first about the meat course and other courses are planned to complement it. . . . beef is by far the most popular of all meats. . . . however pork is usually cheaper. Lamb is the most difficult to find at the market. . . . but chicken is plentiful and poultry raising in Georgia is a big business. Turkey and duck are not quite so popular. . . . but mighty good eating just the same. . . . Quail and other game birds are a little harder to come by. Whichever bird you choose to cook, we think you'll enjoy the recipes for preparing them. . . . on the following pages. . . . along with some favorite beef, pork and lamb recipes. . . . as well as delectable fish recipes.

From the meat house, take two pounds of chuck steak or roast. . . . according to Irene Du Bose, University of Georgia Home Economist. . . . and that's the beginning of a meal.

COUNTRY STEAK WITH ONIONS

2 lbs. chuck steak or roast
1 cup sliced onions
1 teaspoon salt
¼ teaspoon pepper
¼ cup flour
½ teaspoon leaf marjoram spice
3 tablespoons shortening
1¼ cups hot water
2 beef bouillion cubes (dissolve in hot water)
1 (6 oz.) can sliced mushrooms, drained
2 tablespoons chopped parsley flakes

Coat surfaces of steak with mixture of flour, salt, pepper, and marjoram. Brown steak well on both sides in hot shortening in a large frypan, with close-fitting lid. Sprinkle any remaining flour mixture over steak. Add 1 cup onions and remaining ingredients. Cover and cook slowly until tender. Serves 6.

John Richardson (of Ridley Bell's "SPORTMANS LODGE" fame) shares this recipe:

PRIME RIB ROAST AT ITS BEST

5 to 6 pound rib roast
Mix: 1 teaspoon Accent
       1 teaspoon paprika
       2 tablespoons Worcestershire sauce
       salt and seasoned pepper to taste
Rub into all sides of roast.
Preheat oven to 500°F. If using heavy roasting pan (like dutch oven bottom), put about one inch ice cream salt in bottom of pan. Place seasoned roast on salt. . . . then begin pouring salt on roast. . . . sprinkling with water lightly. . . . just wet enough to make it stick together. . . . keep adding salt until you have built a wall around roast, on top and well upon sides. . . . keep sprinkling lightly with water. . . . but not enough to have water standing in pan!!!
Place UNCOVERED in oven. . . . cook:
       12 minutes per lb. for medium done
       15 minutes per lb. for well done
Salt will form a thick covering which you will need to crack off before removing from pan to serve.

When the Reynolds Metals Company came out with "Brown-In-Bags"... they made modern cooking ten times easier! However, cooking foods wrapped in flexible material goes back to the early oriental cultures... wrapping foods in leaves to hold in flavor and moisture. We also know that poultry and fish were cooked in parchment paper... and many other things have been cooked in brown bags... but this plastic Brown-In-Bag designed especially for oven cooking has opened up a whole new world for the cook. It does away with pre-browning, basting, and the usual oven cleaning from splattering! We'd like to share a couple of impressive recipes from the Director of Home Economics for Reynolds.

FRUITED POT ROAST

1 tablespoon flour
3-4 lbs. beef pot roast
½ cup finely chopped onion
½ cup chopped carrots
1 package (11 oz.) mixed dried
    fruit (1¾ cups)
1 clove garlic, pressed
1 cup apple juice

Preheat oven to 350°F. Shake 1 tablespoon flour in family size (14" x 20") Brown-In-Bag and place in two-inch deep roasting pan. Trim excess fat from roast, leaving only a thin layer. Place roast in bag. Arrange onions, carrots, and fruit on and around the roast. Press garlic into apple juice; pour over roast. Close bag with twist tie and make six ½" slits in top. Cook 2-2½ hours or until tested tender. This same recipe may be cooked in a covered roasting pan, but increase cooking time 30 minutes. Serves 6.

ONE STEP SHORT RIBS

½ cup flour
½ teaspoon salt
⅛ teaspoon pepper
3 lbs. short ribs, cut in serving
    size pieces
1 onion, sliced
1 green pepper, sliced
½ cup water
1 tablespoon Worcestershire sauce

Preheat oven to 325°F. Place small size (10" x 16") Brown-In-Bag in two-inch deep roasting pan. Combine flour, salt, and pepper. Rub ribs with seasoned flour; place in bag. Add onion, green pepper. Combine water and Worcestershire sauce and pour over meat. Close bag with twist tie and make six ½-inch slits in top. Cook 2-2½ hours or until tested tender. (Increase cooking time 30 minutes if using covered baking dish.) 4 servings.

BARBECUED SHORT RIBS

1 tablespoon flour
4 lbs. short ribs
1/3 cup catsup
2 tablespoons molasses
1 tablespoon lemon juice
2 teaspoons dry mustard
1/4 teaspoon chili powder
1 clove garlic, pressed
1/2 cup water
1 teaspoon Hickory Smoke

Preheat oven to 350°F. Shake 1 tablespoon flour in small size (10" x 16") Brown-In-Bag and place in two-inch deep roasting pan. Trim excess fat from short ribs. Place ribs in bag and turn to coat ribs with flour in bag. Combine remaining ingredients; add to bag. Turn the bag again to cover short ribs with sauce. Close bag with twist tie and make six half-inch slits in top. Cook 2-2½ hours or until tested tender. (Increase cooking time 30 minutes if using a baking dish with its own cover or heavy-duty foil cover.)

WEST COUNTRY FLANK STEAK

1 flank steak, about 1½ lbs.
1 onion, thinly sliced
1 teaspoon fresh grated lemon
    peel
1/2 cup fresh squeezed lemon juice
2 tablespoons sugar
1/2 teaspoon salt
1/2 teaspoon oregano, crushed
1/8 teaspoon coarse black pepper
2 tablespoons soy sauce
1 tablespoon butter

Trim any fat or membrane from steak. With knife, score steak 1/8 inch deep on both sides in diamond design. Layer half of onions in plastic bag or glass dish. Place steak on top of onions; cover with remaining onions. Thoroughly combine remaining ingredients, except butter; pour over steak and onions. Marinate 2 to 3 hours or overnight in refrigerator, turning several times. Remove steak from marinade; wipe partially dry with paper towel. Drain onions and reserve. Place steak on cold broiler pan, 3 to 5 inches from source of heat in preheated broiler. Broil 3 to 5 minutes on each side. Meanwhile, saute onions in butter until soft. To serve, cut steak across grain in very thin slices; top with onions.

BARBECUED RUMP ROAST

5 to 6 lb. boneless round rump roast
Mix together:
3 cups vinegar
3 cups water
3 medium onions, sliced
2 medium lemons, sliced
16 whole cloves
10 whole black peppercorns
5 bay leaves
2 tablespoons salt

Put meat in marinade, turning to coat well. Cover and put in refrigerator two or three days, turning occasionally. Drain the meat and reserve the marinade. Place roast in shallow roasting pan and bake at 325°F. for 2 to 3 hours depending on desired doneness. Baste roast with reserved marinade during last 30 minutes of cooking time. Let stand for at least 15 minutes before slicing. Serves 10.

CORNED BEEF

2 tablespoons flour
3 lbs. corned beef
1 onion, sliced
1 cup water
½ teaspoon thyme
1 bay leaf, crumbled
2 cloves
1 stalk celery with leaves, cut up
1 small carrot, sliced

Preheat oven to 300°F. Shake 2 tablespoons flour in small size (10" x 16") Brown-In-Bag and place in 2-inch deep roasting pan. Place corned beef in bag. Add remaining ingredients. Close bag with twist tie and make six half-inch slits in top. Cook 3½-4 hours or until tested tender. (May be cooked in covered roasting pan. Add 30 minutes to cooking time.) 5-6 servings.

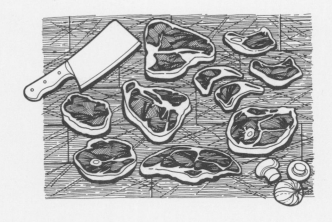

From the hills of Tennessee . . . . comes this recipe . . . . for

BEEF TENDERLOIN

Lard a 3 lb. beef tenderloin with bits of bacon.
Rub salt and pepper to taste into the meat.
Add: 1 chopped carrot
   1 slice of bacon
   1 bay leaf
   2 whole cloves
   pinch of allspice
Cover and bake at 450°F. for 30 minutes, basting often. Bake a longer time if the tenderloin you use is heavier. Serve this with mushroom sauce.

MUSHROOM SAUCE

Add to the brown gravy ¼ can mushrooms and 1 tablespoon lemon juice. Mix 1 tablespoon cornstarch with a little water, add to gravy and stir until lightly thick.

Tenderloin is one of the most expensive cuts of beef, but also one of the most delicious. Here's our best recipe . . . .

BEEF TENDERLOIN WITH GRAVY

4 beef tenderloin steaks (½" thick)
1 tablespoon butter
2 tablespoons catsup
¼ cup brandy
½ cup sour cream
¼ teaspoon salt
1 teaspoon Worcestershire sauce
⅛ teaspoon Tabasco sauce
⅛ teaspoon ground thyme

If you have a heavy cast iron skillet, this is a good place to use it, if not, any heavy skillet will do. Brown steaks in the melted butter, turning often until desired doneness. (About 12 minutes for well done). Remove from heat, pour half the brandy over the meat, then place steaks on warm platter to keep them warm. Combine sour cream, catsup, salt, Worcestershire, Tabasco, thyme, and remaining brandy. Add to same skillet where you cooked the steaks. Heat until hot through. Spoon over steaks and pass the remainder. Serves 4.

PEPPER FLANK STEAK

1 tablespoon flour
2-2½ lbs. flank steak
2 green peppers
1 tablespoon soy sauce
1 beef bouillon cube, crushed
1 teaspoon salt
½ teaspoon sugar
1 clove garlic, pressed
½ teaspoon ginger
1 can (16 oz.) tomatoes

Preheat oven to 375°F. Shake 1 tablespoon flour in small size (10" x 16") Brown-In-Bag and place in two-inch deep roasting pan. Slice steak diagonally as for london broil. Place in oven bag. Cut green peppers into strips; place on meat. Combine remaining ingredients and pour over steak. Close bag with twist tie and make six one-half inch slits in top. Cook 1½-2 hours or until tested tender. Increase cooking time 30 minutes if using a covered baking dish.

There is a great group of people who have held their conventions at Callaway Gardens for several years. . . . the Georgia Cattleman's Association. Their Auxiliary, the Georgia Cowbells, has collected some mighty tasty beef recipes. . . . try them for yourself. This one from Luchow's in New York is known all over the country. . . .

SAUERBRATEN

3 to 3½ lbs. beef round or rump
4 bay leaves
½ teaspoon peppercorns
8 whole cloves
2 medium onions, sliced
1 small carrot, minced
1 stalk celery, chopped
1½ cups red wine vinegar
2½ cups water
¼ cup butter

Rub meat with 1 teaspoon of salt and ½ teaspoon of pepper. Place in deep earthenware crock or ovenware glass bowl; add spices and vegetables. Heat vinegar and water to boiling; pour hot over meat. Cool. Cover bowl; refrigerate. Marinate at least 48 hours, turning twice a day. When ready to cook, remove meat from marinade and dry with paper towels. Melt butter in Dutch oven and brown meat all over. Strain marinade and pour over meat. Cover tightly; simmer slowly 2½ to 3 hours until fork tender. Remove to warmed platter. Slice and serve warm. Serves 6.

No heartier dish ever graced the table in the North or the South than this old recipe for. . . .

BROWN BEEF STEW

3 lbs. stew beef, trimmed of all fat and cut into ½" cubes
carrots and potatoes - half and half to equal bulk of meat - cut in ½" pieces
1 green pepper, very finely chopped
2 carrots finely grated
½ lb. fresh mushrooms, separate caps and stems
1 can consomme & 2 cans water
1 beef bouillon cube
salt, pepper, paprika, garlic salt
Kitchen Bouquet or other brown meat sauce
¼ cup wine (Burgundy)

Sprinkle meat with salt, pepper, and paprika and brown in butter in bottom of a deep pressure cooker. When meat is fairly well browned, add green pepper and the finely grated carrots. Watch the pan closely, stirring with a wooden spoon so the vegetables do not burn. Add potatoes, carrots, consomme and bouillon cube to meat. Follow cooking instructions for beef stew given in your pressure cooker booklet. Saute mushrooms in butter in a large frying pan; transfer to another pan; Make a roux of butter and flour in the first pan and cook with the juice from the pressure cooker until it begins to thicken; add a little Kitchen Bouquet. . . just a drop or two. Add mushrooms, meat and vegetables to the sauce. Add more Kitchen Bouquet until a rich brown color is reached. Carefully dip and turn and stir the ingredients in the pan with the wooden spoon until you are satisfied with the color and the sauce is blended with all ingredients. Remove from fire. Cook. Stir in wine. Store in refrigerator for 24 hours. Return to the copper pan, reheat, stirring carefully, and serve from the pan with crusty bread and a green salad.

Many thanks to the cook who handed this recipe down. . . .

LARRY'S OVEN STEW

1½ lb. sirloin tips
1 cup sliced carrots
1 cup sliced celery
1 cup sliced onions
2 tablespoons tapioca
1 teaspoon salt
½ teaspoon seasoned salt
1 teaspoon Worcestershire sauce

Mix all of the above ingredients in bowl and put into a deep, well greased covered casserole. Pour 1¼ cups tomato juice over all. Cover tightly. Cook 4½ hours at 250°F. Serve over rice or noodles.

BEEF CASSEROLE WITH CORN TOPPING

1 medium onion, minced
2 tablespoons shortening
2 lbs. ground beef
2 tablespoons flour
2½ tablespoons chili powder
3 teaspoons salt
½ cup seedless raisins
1 can (17 oz.) cream style corn
2 eggs, well beaten
3 tablespoons sugar
1 cup milk

Cook onion in shortening 2 to 3 minutes; add beef and cook until meat loses its color. Mix flour, chili powder, 2 teaspoons salt, and pepper with ½ cup water and stir into meat. Cook, stirring until thickened. Remove from heat and fold in raisins. Put in 3 quart casserole about 3 inches deep. Mix corn, remaining salt, raw eggs, 2 tablespoons sugar, and the milk in a saucepan. Cook over medium heat until thickened, stirring often. Pour corn mixture over meat mixture in casserole and sprinkle with one tablespoon sugar. Bake in 350°F. oven for 30-40 minutes. Serves 6 to 8 people.

This recipe is an old one. . . . probably handed down from our English friends who considered it a main dish. . . .

MEAT PIE

4 tablespoons cooking fat
3 tablespoons chopped onion
2 tablespoons chopped green pepper
½ cup diced celery
1 cup diced cooked meat
4 tablespoons flour
2 cups milk or meat stock
½ cup diced cooked carrots

Slightly brown onion, pepper, celery, and meat in cooking fat, stirring constantly. Add flour slowly, stirring constantly, until brown. Add remaining ingredients. Heat thoroughly. Pour into shallow, well-oiled baking dish. Cover with biscuits. Bake in hot (450°F.) oven about 15 minutes. Serves 6.

GROUND BEEF CASSEROLE

1 large onion, chopped
2 tablespoons butter
1 lb. ground beef
2 tablespoons flour
1½ teaspoons salt
¼ teaspoon pepper
1 tall can evaporated milk,
    undiluted
2 cups cooked peas
¼ cup diced red pimento
1 can your favorite refrigerated
    biscuits

Saute onion slowly in butter 3 minutes. Add ground beef; cook over low heat until brown, breaking up meat with fork as it cooks. Blend in flour, salt, pepper; stir in evaporated milk, peas and pimento. Heat, but do not boil; simmer 3 minutes, stirring constantly. Turn hot meat mixture into 2 quart casserole. Arrange biscuits on top of meat. Bake in hot oven (450°F.) 20 to 25 minutes, or until biscuits are golden brown.

From the Corning Ware Kitchens came this Beef Casserole....a complete meal....you might want to serve a green salad, but no bread or other vegetable....

WESTERN SUPPER CASSEROLE

2 lbs. lean ground beef
1½ cups chopped onion
2 cloves garlic, minced
2 (15 oz.) cans Hunt's Tomato
    Sauce with Tomato Bits
2 (16 oz.) cans whole kernel corn,
    drained
1 (4 oz.) can sliced ripe olives
2 tablespoons chili powder
2 teaspoons salt
2 eggs, beaten
¾ cup yellow corn meal
1 cup milk
1½ cups grated sharp Cheddar
cheese

Brown beef in skillet; add onion and garlic. Cook until onion is soft. Drain fat. Add tomato sauce, corn, olives, chili powder, and 1 teaspoon salt. Cover; simmer 15 minutes. Pour into 12¼"x10¼"x 2¼" open roaster. In a small bowl, combine corn meal, milk, eggs, remaining salt, and 1 cup cheese; pour over filling. Sprinkle remaining cheese over top. Bake at 350°F. 40 to 50 minutes.
Makes 10 to 12 servings.

Here is an old Southern family recipe for meat loaf which can be wrapped in heavy-duty foil. . . .sauce and all. . . .and frozen until needed. We recommend using it within 4 to 6 weeks. . . .

A SAVORY MEAT LOAF

2 lbs. ground beef	Mix ingredients together well.
2 teaspoons salt	Shape into 1 large loaf or 2 small
1 tall can Pet milk	loaves and place in lightly greased
1 cup 3-minute oats	baking dish. Place in 350°F. oven
1 finely chopped large onion	while making sauce.
½ teaspoon coarsely ground black pepper	
Sauce:	
1½ cups finely chopped onion	Saute in butter.
2 finely chopped large green peppers	
1½ cups finely chopped celery	
Pinch of salt	
3 tablespoons butter	
1 32-oz. bottle tomato catsup	Add to onion, pepper and celery
½ catsup bottle of water (2 cups)	mixture.
1 medium size can tomato sauce	
3 tablespoons Worcestershire sauce	Heat to boiling and pour over meat loaf. Continue cooking for 1
1 teaspoon Tabasco	hour basting with sauce from pan about every 15 minutes.

SPAGHETTI MEAT SAUCE

⅓ cup olive oil	Heat olive oil in large sauce pan;
3 large onions	add thinly sliced onions, green
2 large green peppers	pepper (chopped). Cook until
2 lbs. ground beef	onions begin to get tender. Add
2 cans tomato paste	ground beef. Cook until it begins
2 cans tomato sauce	to turn color. Add salt, black
2 tablespoons Tabasco	pepper, crushed red peppers,
2 tablespoons Worcestershire sauce	chili powder, tomato sauce, tomato paste, Tabasco, Worcester-
½ tablespoons crushed red pepper	shire, canned tomatoes and mushrooms. Bring to boiling point and
4 tablespoons chili powder	turn down heat to simmer.
1 teaspoon salt	Simmer two hours.
1 teaspoon black pepper	
1 can whole tomatoes	
2 cans whole mushrooms	

We are grateful to the Colonists for recording in their diaries, where it could be handed from generation to generation, this unusual recipe for. . . .

BEEF ROYALE

We copied it exactly as it appeared in the 1700's.

Take a sirloin of beef, or a large rump, bone it and beat it very well. Then lard it with bacon, season it all over with salt, pepper, mace, cloves, and nutmeg (all beat fine), some lemon peel cut small, and some sweet herbs; in the mean time, make a strong broth of the bones, take a piece of butter with a little flour, brown it, put in the beef, keep it turning often till it is brown, then strain the broth, put all together into a pot, put in a bay leaf, a few truffles, and some ox palates cut small; cover it close, and let it stew 'til it is tender, take out the beef, skim off all the fat, pour in a pint of claret, some fried oysters, an anchovy, and some gerkins-shred small; boil all together, put in the beef to warm. Thicken your sauce with a piece of butter rolled in flour, or mushroom powder, or burnt butter. Lay your meat in the dish, pour the sauce over it, and send it to the table. This may be eaten either hot or cold.

Note: This stew had no vegetables in it except pot herbs and onions; potatoes and carrots were not added to stews until the 19th century. This beef is simple enough for a country meal, or elegant enough for a formal dinner.

Another beef recipe which dates back to immigrant groups. . . . straight from England. . . . it found its way from the New England States into the Deep South. It is. . . .

BEEF WITH YORKSHIRE PUDDING

8 lb. standing beef rib roast

Season with a mixture of salt, pepper and some seasoning salt. Rub well into all sides of the roast. Put in uncovered shallow roasting pan. Cook at 325°F.: 3½ hours for rare, 4 hours for medium, 4½ hours for well-done. Take meat from pan, cover and keep warm. Increase oven temperature to 400°F. for cooking pudding.

YORKSHIRE PUDDING

4 eggs
2 cups milk
⅛ teaspoon black pepper
2 cups all-purpose flour
1 teaspoon salt

Beat eggs with milk. Add salt and pepper to flour, and mix into egg mixture (a good way is to use your sifter and beat well after each addition.) Beat two minutes by hand or with mixer. Take ¼ cup of meat drippings and pour half of it into each of two 9"x9"x2" baking pans. Pour half the batter into each pan. Bake at 400°F. for 30 minutes. Serve hot with roast. Serves 12.

People brought up on the farm will always remember the wonderful foods that came out of the farm kitchen. From the first pioneer settlers, we learned to salt and smoke meat, but no cured meat ever did or ever will outshine country ham with redeye gravy, and we share this good recipe with you. . . .

COUNTRY HAM WITH REDEYE GRAVY

Cut three ½-inch thick country ham slices (or fully cooked ham) slices in half. Trim the fat from the ham slices, reserving trimmings. In skillet, cook trimming until crisp. Discard trimmings and brown the ham on both sides in the hot fat, 5 to 6 minutes per side. Remove ham to warm platter. Stir ⅔ cup boiling water and 1 teaspoon instant coffee powder into the drippings in skillet. If ham is mild-cured, add a few drops liquid smoke. Cook, scraping pan to remove crusty bits for 2 to 3 minutes. Serve warm gravy over ham slices. Serve ham with Speckled Heart Grits. Makes 6 servings.

COUNTRY BAKED HAM

8 lb. ham
3 quarts sweet cider
2 cups raisins
2 cups maple sugar*
2 teaspoons dry mustard
1 teaspoon powdered cloves
½ cup water

Simmer ham in cider for two hours. Drain, skin ham, and cover it with paste made from maple sugar, mustard, cloves, and water. Place it in baking pan, pour cider liquid over it, add raisins to pan, and bake 2½ hours at 325°F. Baste frequently. Make thickened gravy of cider raisin drippings. Serves 16.

*Brown sugar may be used in place of maple sugar. However, maple sugar gives it an entirely different taste.

SUGARED HAM

1 slice ham, one inch thick
1 cup dark brown sugar,
    more if needed
4 cloves
½ cup cider
equal parts of vinegar and water—
    to cover ham for soaking

Trim ham and place in sufficient tart vinegar and water to cover well. Let soak two hours. Drain and wipe well. Cover with sugar, rub in well, do this on both sides, place into a baking dish, pour over the half cup of cider, stick in cloves, cover top with more sugar. Bake slowly for two hours. Remove from pan, make sauce of drippings, using flour and water with sauces to season well. Serve the sauce in separate dish.

A long time friend from the Sunkist Kitchens gave us her secret for a picture perfect ham. . . . note the **do's** and **don'ts** and use her glaze. It's simple and **simply** delicious! I wouldn't add a thing.

Here's the secret to picture perfect ham:
Follow these simple rules for perfect, juicy baked ham every time!
Place ham on rack in **shallow** pan. **Do not** score or remove outer rind. **Do not** season or baste. Refer to all-purpose cookbook for the roasting chart that recommends oven temperature of 325°F. Select the length of time suggested for the kind and weight of ham you are cooking. (Follow label on canned hams.) About 40 minutes before ham is done, remove from oven. Transfer to cutting board and cut away outer rind, leaving an even layer of fat about ¼-inch thick. Score surface in diamond design; stud with whole cloves, if desired. Return to rack, brush or spoon entire surface with glaze. Return to oven and continue baking 40 minutes longer, basting with glaze two or three times.

FRESH ORANGE GLAZE FOR HAM

3½ tablespoons coarsely grated orange peel (2 Sunkist oranges)
½ cup freshly squeezed orange juice
1 cup firmly packed brown sugar
2 teaspoons dry mustard
2 tablespoons prepared mustard

In small saucepan, thoroughly combine all ingredients; boil hard five minutes stirring constantly. **Cool** to room temperature. Follow glazing instructions above.

And here's a bit of unusual treatment for a ham loaf. . . .

GLAZED HAM LOAF

2 lbs. ground smoked ham
2 lbs. ground fresh pork
2½ cups graham crackers, crushed
4 eggs
1½ cups milk
1 can tomato soup
1 cup brown sugar
½ cup water
½ cup vinegar
½ cup mustard
½ teaspoon salt

Mix first 5 ingredients together. Form into loaf and place in baking dish. Mix remaining ingredients together for sauce. Bake 2 hours in 300°F. oven. Baste loaf to keep loaf moist. Sauce will form a rich thick glaze. Serves 8 - 10.

Ham can be cooked so many ways. It is a traditional dish in many lands, but the one we'd like to share with you now comes from Britian. A pretty tasty idea for the holidays.... it's called....

STUFFED HAM

Some of the things which make this dish different is the use of celery, sage, and honey.... items to be found in any country kitchen.

1 fully cooked ham, weighing
    about 12 lbs.
1 medium-size onion,
    chopped (½ cup)
½ cup chopped celery
½ cup (1 stick) butter or
    margarine
5 cups soft bread crumbs
    (10 slices)
1 tablespoon leaf sage, crumbled
½ cup honey
2 tablespoons lemon juice
watercress

Place ham in a large deep roasting pan; pour in water to a depth of 2 inches. Heat to boiling; cover. Simmer 1 hour. Cool slightly, them remove ham to a large shallow pan. Trim off rind, if any, and excess fat, leaving a layer about ¼ inch thick. While ham simmers, saute onion and celery in butter or margarine until soft in a medium-size frying pan. Pour over bread crumbs and sage in a large bowl; toss lightly to mix. Turn ham, fat side up; make 2" deep cuts, 1½" apart, lenghtwise into meat. Press stuffing mixture into cuts. Bake in slow oven (325°F.) 30 minutes. Mix honey and lemon juice in a cup; brush part over ham between stuffing rows. Continue baking, brushing every 15 minutes with remaining honey mixture, 45 minutes, or until richly glazed. Place ham on large serving platter; garnish with watercress. Makes 8 servings, with enough left over for the next day. Total baking time: 1 hour and 15 minutes.

Luther Way, a gentleman cook, of Swainsboro, GA, says this recipe for fresh ham is the best he'd ever tasted (and we agree!). He is the fourth generation to use this recipe for. . . .

BOILED FRESH PORK HAM

Use heavy kettle with close fitting lid. . . .
For best results, use small pork ham. . . . not over five pounds. Wash the ham well. . . . cut the small shank off if you don't have a large pot. Sprinkle with salt all over. Put ham in pot and **cover with water.** Bring water to boil, then turn heat down to medium. (Allow 20 minutes per pound.) Taste occasionally to see if broth is salty enough. Cook on medium heat until tender. (To test for doneness. . . . insert a sharp fork or hat pin in the thickest part on under side. If the juice is pink, it is done. If it is red, it isn't done, and must be cooked longer.) Be sure to cook with moderate heat because if it is boiled too hard, the outside will tear, but the inside will not be done.
When done, remove to large serving platter. Make several deep cuts all over ham, and fill holes with finely chopped onion. Pepper generously **all over** with coarsely ground black pepper. Wrap in aluminum foil and (or several thickness of cheese cloth) store in refrigerator until needed. Some like to add ½ cup molasses and ½ cup vinegar in the water when boiling.

Hearty winter dish. . . . Let a lemon make the difference!

PEPPY PORK DINNER

4 pork loin chops (about 1½ lbs.)
¼ cup flour
1½ teaspoons salt
⅛ teaspoon pepper
1 to 2 tablespoons shortening
4 medium potatoes, quartered (about 1¼ lbs.)
6 carrots, quartered (about 1 lb.)
2 small onions, quartered
½ cup water
juice of 1 fresh lemon
1 tablespoon sugar
1 bay leaf, crushed
¼ teaspoon celery seed

Coat pork chops with mixture of flour, 1 teaspoon salt and pepper. In a heavy saucepot, brown chops in shortening; pour off fat. Arrange vegetables over chops. In small bowl, combine remaining ½ teaspoon salt, water, lemon juice, sugar, bay leaf, and celery seed. Pour over chops and vegetables. Cover and simmer for 45 to 50 minutes until pork chops and vegetables are tender. Makes 4 servings.

Top of the list of that very favorite southern dish . . . . is our . . . .

STUFFED PORK CHOPS

6 thick (1") pork chops
2 cups toasted bread crumbs
2 tablespoons melted butter
1 small onion, grated
1 teaspoon salt
1/4 teaspoon pepper
1/4 teaspoon ground sage
1/2 cup evaporated milk, undiluted

Have butcher cut slits in pork chops for dressing. Blend crumbs, onion, and seasonings. Stuff chops with dressing and fasten with small skewers or tie with cord to hold stuffing in pork chops. Brown chops in frying pan. Arrange in baking dish; add evaporated milk. Cover casserole for the first 25 minutes (50 minutes at 350°F.); then uncover for remaining time.

Note: if you use salt and pepper on pork chops before cooking, it has a tendency to make the chops tough.

PORK CHOPS WITH BROWNED RICE

4 pork chops
2 tablespoons shortening
3 teaspoons salt
1 cup uncooked rice
2 cups canned tomatoes
1 1/2 cups water
1/4 teaspoon pepper
1/2 cup chopped green pepper
1/2 cup chopped onion

Brown pork chops in shortening. Remove from pan. Season with salt (1 tsp.). Wash rice. Brown in shortening, stirring constantly. Add tomatoes, water, pepper, onion, and remaining salt (2 tsp.). Lay chops on top of this mixture. Cover. Cook over simmer flame for 45 minutes or until rice is tender.

PORK CHOP SKILLET

6 pork chops (1 1/2 lbs.)
1/4 cup sliced green onion
1 can (10 1/2 oz.) Campbell's Condensed Golden Mushroom Soup
1/3 cup sour cream
1/4 cup water
2 teaspoons prepared mustard
1 package (10 oz.) frozen lima beans
2 tablespoons chopped pimiento

In skillet, brown chops and cook until tender (use shortening, if necessary). Pour off fat. Add soup, sour cream, water and mustard. Cover; cook over low heat for 30 minutes. Stir now and then. Add beans and pimiento. Cook 15 minutes more or until meat and vegetables are tender. Stir now and then. Makes 4 servings.

LOIS McCOSH'S SAUSAGE-ONION SNACKS

1 pound fresh mushrooms
1 pound bulk pork sausage
1 large onion, finely chopped
2 cups Bisquick Baking Mix
3/4 cup milk
3 eggs
1 tablespoon caraway or poppy
   seed
1 1/2 cups dairy sour cream
1/4 teaspoon salt
paprika

Heat oven to 350°. Grease baking pan, 13x9x2 inches. Cook and stir sausage and onion over medium heat until sausage is brown, drain. Mix baking mix, milk and one egg. Spread in pan. Sprinkle with caraway or poppy seed. Top with sausage mixture. Mix sour cream, salt and remaining egg. Pour evenly over sausage. Sprinkle with paprika. Bake in uncovered pan until set, 25-30 minutes. Cut into rectangles. . . . about 2x1 1/2 inches. Makes about 32 pieces.

SAUSAGE-APPLE RING WITH CHEESE SCRAMBLED EGGS

2 lbs. bulk sausage
1 1/2 cups cracker crumbs
2 eggs, slightly beaten
1/2 cup milk
1/4 cup minced onion
1 cup finely chopped apple
canned apricots (garnish)
parsley (garnish)

Combine all ingredients for sausage ring and mix thoroughly with a fork. Press lightly in a greased 6-cup ring mold. Turn out in a shallow baking pan. Bake in moderate oven (350°F) for about 1 hour. Drain excess fat from pan. The ring may be partially baked the day before for 30 minutes and then finished the morning of the brunch. To serve, fill center of sausage ring with scrambled eggs to which you have added a little grated cheese. Sprinkle eggs with paprika. Garnish platter with broiled apricot halves and parsley. Makes 8 servings.

Some people object to the sometimes unpleasant taste of lamb. If the rind of the lamb is scrubbed with a bit of cooking soda then rinsed with cold water, it will eliminate the unpleasant taste.

LAMB STEW

1½ lbs. shoulder, breast or flank
1½ cups diced carrots
1 cup diced celery
1½ cups diced potatoes
2 tablespoons diced onion
¼ cup canned tomatoes
pepper
1½ teaspoons salt
¼ cup cooking fat

Dice lamb. Brown in cooking fat, or fat from lamb. Cover with water. Add salt. Simmer until meat is tender.... add vegetables. Season to taste. Cover. Simmer for 30 minutes. If desired, drop dumplings may be cooked with the stew. Six servings.

This recipe for Broiled Lamb Chops dates back to the Franciscan Missions in the far West, so I guess we'd called it....

WESTERN BROILED LAMB CHOPS

6 lamb chops (½ to ¾-inch thick)
For marinade:
½ cup white wine
¼ cup cooking oil
¼ cup finely chopped onion
¼ cup finely chopped parsley
½ teaspoon salt
⅛ teaspoon pepper
⅛ teaspoon crushed red pepper
1 clove of garlic, finely chopped

Make marinade of listed ingredients. Place lamb chops in shallow baking dish.... do not crowd. Pour marinade over and let stand 2 hours at room temperature or overnight in the refrigerator. Have marinade completely cover chops or spoon over several times. Remove lamb chops and reserve marinade. Place lamb chops on rack of broiler pan, brush with marinade. Broil for 6 to 8 minutes per side.... then turn chops and brush with marinade.... broil 6 to 8 minutes longer.... If you like lamb, you'll like these chops.... serves 6.

LAMB CUTLETS

2 cups finely chopped cold cooked lamb
2 teaspoons lemon juice
⅛ teaspoon pepper
1 cup thick white sauce
1 teaspoon minced parsley
½ teaspoon salt
1 egg, slightly beaten

Combine lamb, white sauce, lemon juice, parsley, and seasonings. Mix thoroughly. Cook. Shape in rounds 2 inches in diameter, and ½ inch thick. Dip in egg and cracker crumbs. Fry in deep fat (385°F.) until brown. Drain on crumpled absorbent paper. Serves 8.

Lois McCosh. . . . well known area caterer shares her recipe for:

ROAST LAMB WITH CHILI PLUM SAUCE

1 (5 to 6 lb.) leg of lamb
5 garlic buds
rosemary
dry white wine
½ cup thinly sliced green onion
6 tablespoons butter
1 (10 oz.) jar plum jam
½ cup chili sauce
¼ cup dry white wine
1 tablespoon lemon juice
1 teaspoon ground allspice
1 teaspoon snipped parsley

Remove thin fat covering from surface of roast. Make thin slits in meat; insert garlic slivers. Moisten meat with wine and sprinkle with rosemary. Place on rack in large roasting pan. Roast, uncovered, in 325°F. oven for 2 to 3 hours, or 'til meat thermometer registers 140° for rare, or 2½ to 3¾ hours for medium (160°). Meanwhile in a medium saucepan, cook onion in butter til tender; stir in jam, chili sauce, wine, lemon juice, and allspice. Bring to boil, stirring constantly. Simmer, uncovered. Stir in parsley. Spoon sauce atop roast; pass remaining sauce.

Lamb may be cooked on gas grill by searing meat directly on grids and then placing in large foil pan. If you do not use rack, add small amount of wine to base of pan.

Don Fabiani, of the Columbus Conventions and Visitors Bureau, adds to country cooking with his original recipe for duck called. . . .

DON'S DUCK BOG

2 wild ducks
2 cloves
2 small onions
2 (1") strips of salt pork
½ teaspoon pepper
1½ teaspoons salt
4 strips bacon
1 cup apple juice
1 cup orange juice
½ cup Harvey's Hunting Port
    Wine
2 tablespoons orange rind
½ teaspoon thyme
3 tablespoons melted butter
1 tablespoon A-1 Steak Sauce

Wash and dry ducks. Stick a clove in each onion and place 1 onion and 1 piece of salt pork in each duck. Season with salt and pepper then cover the breast with bacon. Place in shallow roasting pan. Mix apple juice, orange juice, wine, orange rind, and thyme. Pour over ducks. Roast for 1 hour (350°F. oven) or until tender. Baste frequently. Five minutes before ducks are done, discard bacon and brush with mixture of butter and A-1 sauce.

ELAINE'S DUCK SUPREME

2 cans cream of mushroom soup
2 wild ducks
4 small onions
1 teaspoon salt
8-10 peppercorns
1 stalk celery
1 teaspoon parsley

Pan boil the ducks with salt, peppercorns, celery, onions, parsley. Remove ducks from broth and cube meat. Place in 2-quart casserole and cover with mushroom soup. Bake in a 350°F. oven for 45 minutes. Serve over wild rice.

ROASTED GLAZED DUCK

4 to 5 lbs. wild ducklings
   (thoroughly cleaned)
½ lemon
½ teaspoon thyme
salt and freshly ground black
   pepper
½ cup honey
2 tablespoons curry powder

Wash duck and dry well. Rub inside and out with cut side of lemon, dry thoroughly. Rub cavity of duck with thyme, and inside and out with salt and pepper. Place on a rack set in a roasting pan and roast in a 325° oven for 35 minutes. With a fork prick the entire surface and roast for 25 more minutes. Mix honey and curry powder until well combined. Remove duck from oven and brush well with some of the honey-curry mixture. Return to oven and roast ½ hour longer, brushing with mixture every 10 minutes or so. (For well-done duck, roast 2 hours in all.) Serve at once, with rice.

Fishing was America's first industry and as far back as 1780, it was recorded that "the greatest delicacy of the fresh water river is the blue catfish." Don't know if you agree. . . .but if you like catfish, you'll love this recipe for. . . .

COUNTRY-FRIED CATFISH

12 pan-dressed catfish (or whiting)
   9 - 12 oz.
2 large eggs, beaten
¼ cup milk
1½ teaspoons salt
¼ teaspoon pepper
1 cup all-purpose flour
1 cup dry bread crumbs
cooking oil for deep frying

Thaw fish, if frozen. Combine eggs, milk, salt, and pepper; mix. Combine and mix flour and crumbs. Dip fish in egg mixture; roll in flour mixture to coat evenly. Fry in deep hot oil, 350°F. 3 to 5 minutes or until fish flakes easily when tested with a fork. Drain on absorbent paper. Serve with hush puppies and tartar sauce. 12 servings.

BAKED STRIPED BASS

Clean 2 striped bass, each weighing 3 lbs., and remove the center bones. Sprinkle the inside with 1 teaspoon salt and ¼ teaspoon white pepper. Saute 2 large onions, peeled and minced, in ¼ cup butter until they are golden and mix them well with 1½ lbs. filet of flounder or sole, ground, 1 teaspoon salt, and ½ teaspoon paprika. Fill the fish with the stuffing. In the bottom of a large shallow baking dish, arrange 1½ lbs. mushrooms, thinly sliced, and 2 large green peppers, seeded, and cut into julienne. Put the fish on the vegetables, sprinkle them with 2 teaspoons salt and ½ teaspoon paprika, and dot with ¼ cup butter. Bake the fish in a moderately hot oven (375°F.) for 45 minutes, or until the flesh flakes easily. Transfer the fish to a platter and keep it warm. Pour the remaining vegetables and juices into a saucepan and stir in a mixture of 1 tablespoon flour and ⅓ cup each of cream and freshly grated Parmesan cheese. Cook the sauce, stirring, until it is thickened. Pour it over the fish and serve immediately.

Here's a way to add zest to ordinary fish fillets. . . . and we thank Hunt-Wesson Kitchens for it. . . . It's called. . . .

CAPTAIN TOM'S FISH BAKE

1 cup chopped onion
½ cup chopped celery and tops
½ cup chopped parsley
1½ lbs. fish fillets
Wesson oil
¾ teaspoon salt
⅛ teaspoon pepper
½ teaspoon paprika
2 (8 oz.) cans Hunt's
   Tomato Sauce with Mushrooms

Combine onion, celery and parsley; arrange in bottom of large, shallow, oiled baking dish. Place fish in overlapping layers over the vegetables. Brush fillets with Wesson oil, sprinkle with salt, pepper and paprika. Bake at 375° for 10 minutes. Pour Hunt's Tomato sauce with Mushrooms over all.
Bake 30 minutes longer or until fish is flaky and sauce bubbles. Makes 4 to 5 servings.

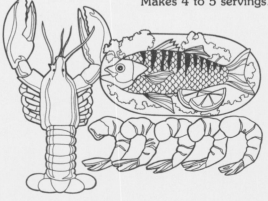

Best recipe for fried oysters you'll ever try.... any Southern cook will give you about this same recipe....

FRIED OYSTERS

These fried oysters have an extra "bit of dash" due to the horseradish used in this recipe.

Select large oysters, drain well, and season with salt, pepper, and lemon juice. On each oyster spread a small bit of horseradish. Dip the oysters in fine crumbs, then in egg beaten slighly with a teaspoon of cold water. Dip again in crumbs and fry in deep hot fat. Drain and serve with catsup or chili sauce. Garnish with lemon slices.

SALMON CROQUETTES

1 (16 oz.) can salmon
3 tablespoons butter or margarine
1/4 cup all-purpose flour
1/2 cup milk
1 tablespoon snipped parsley
2 teaspoon lemon juice
1 teaspoon grated onion
dash paprika
dash ground nutmeg
1 cup fine dry bread crumbs
1 beaten egg
2 tablespoons water

Drain salmon, reserving 1/2 cup liquid. Remove bones and skin; flake meat. Melt butter in saucepan. Blend in flour. Add milk and reserved liquid. Cook and stir 'til thickened and bubbly. Cook and stir 1 minute longer. Add next 5 ingredients, 1/4 teaspoon salt and dash of pepper. Stir in salmon; chill.

With wet hands, shape salmon mixture into 8 balls, using about 1/4 cup for each. Roll in crumbs. Shape balls into cones, handling lightly so crumbs remain on outside. Dip into mixture of beaten egg and water; roll in crumbs again. Fry a few at a time in deep, hot fat (350°F.) till brown and hot about 2 1/2 to 3 minutes. Drain on paper toweling. Serves 4.

SHRIMP COCKTAIL

3/4 cup chili sauce
4 tablespoons lemon juice
2 tablespoons prepared horseradish
2 teaspoons Worcestershire sauce
1/2 teaspoon grated onion
1/2 teaspoon Tabasco
salt
shelled cooked shrimp, chilled
lettuce

Combine chili sauce, lemon juice, horseradish, Worcestershire sauce, onion, and Tabasco. Mix well; add salt to taste. Chill.

Arrange 4 shelled, cooked shrimp in each lettuce-lined cocktail glass. Spoon about 2 tablespoons chilled cocktail sauce atop each. Makes enough sauce for 8 - 10 cocktails.

PICKLED SHRIMP

½ cup salad oil
½ cup lime juice
2 tablespoons vinegar
1 tablespoon snipped chives
1½ teaspoons salt
½ teaspoon dried dillweed
3 drops Tabasco
2 teaspoons capers
2 lbs. shelled shrimp, cooked

Combine oil, lime juice, vinegar, chives, salt, dill, Tabasco, and capers. Add shrimp; toss. Chill several hours, stirring occasionally. Drain and serve with wooden picks.

SHRIMP CREOLE

2½ lbs. medium frozen shrimp, peeled and deveined
1 cup chopped onion
1 cup chopped green pepper
½ clove garlic, minced
½ cup cooking oil or margarine
⅔ cup all-purpose flour
1½ tablespoons salt
1 teaspoon pepper
5 cups canned tomatoes
¾ lb. uncooked rice

Thaw shrimp. Cook onion, green pepper, and garlic in cooking oil until tender, but not brown. Blend in flour, salt, and pepper. Add tomatoes and cook until thickened stirring occasionally. Add shrimp, and simmer 3 to 5 minutes. Cook rice according to package directions. Portion: ¾ cup shrimp creole over ½ cup rice. Serves 12.

A recipe for pan size fish. . . . as recommended by Florida Department of Natural Resources. . . .

SMOKED HERBED FISH

2 lbs. fish fillets, fresh or frozen
1 (8 oz.) bottle Italian salad dressing
2 teaspoons salt
2 cups finely-crushed herb-seasoned stuffing mix
½ teaspoon oregano
¼ cup chopped parsley

Thaw frozen fish. Cut into serving-size portions. Place fish in a single layer in a shallow baking dish. Pour Italian dressing over fish and let stand 30 minutes. Remove fish from sauce and sprinkle with salt. Combine herb-seasoned stuffing mix, oregano, and parsley. Roll fish in herbed mixture. Place fish on well-greased grill in baking dish. Cook in a slow oven (200°F.) for approximately 1 hour or until fish flakes easily when tested with a fork. Makes 6 servings.

This is a dependable casserole. . . . easy to prepare and a. . . .

FISHERMAN'S DELIGHT

½ cup butter or margarine
¼ cup thinly sliced scallions
1½ cups sliced celery
1 (3 oz.) can sliced mushrooms,
    drained, reserving liquid
⅓ cup all-purpose flour
1 pint light cream or dairy
    Half and Half
¾ teaspoon salt
⅛ teaspoon ground black pepper
1 (7 oz.) can tuna, drained
1 (1 lb.) package frozen haddock
    fillets, thawed, very well
    drained and cut into bite-size
    pieces
1 (4 oz.) jar sliced pimentos,
    drained
25 Ritz crackers, finely rolled
    (approx. 1 cup crumbs)
3 tablespoons grated Parmesan
    cheese
lemon slices and parsley sprigs
    optional

Melt ¼ cup butter or margarine in large saucepan; add next 3 ingredients and cook 5 minutes. Remove from pan. In same pan, heat 2 tablespoons margarine; blend in flour. Gradually add mushroom liquid and light cream, blending until smooth. Cook and stir constantly over medium heat until mixture thickens. Cook one minute. Do not boil. Remove from heat. Add next five ingredients and mushroom mixture. Blend well. Pour into greased individual casseroles. Combine Ritz cracker crumbs and cheese. Add remaining 2 tablespoons margarine, melted. Blend thoroughly. Sprinkle evenly over casseroles. Refrigerate until ready to heat and serve. If chilled for any length of time, let stand at room temperature before baking. Bake in a preheated 350°F. oven 25 to 30 minutes or until golden. Makes 4 (¾ cup) servings.

QUICK 'N' EASY PERCH

2 lbs. perch fillets, fresh or frozen
¼ cup butter or margarine,
    melted
2 tablespoons lemon juice
2 tablespoons chopped parsley
½ teaspoon salt
⅛ teaspoon pepper
paprika
lemon wedges

Thaw fish, if frozen, and skin fillets and place on a greased broil-and-serve platter, 16" x 10". Combine remaining ingredients except paprika and lemon wedges. Pour over fillets and let stand for 30 minutes. Broil about 4 inches from source of heat for 8 to 10 minutes or until fish flakes easily when tested with a fork. Sprinkle with paprika. Serve with lemon wedges. Serves six.

Cacklin' Good Receipts from the Chicken Yard

CACKLIN' GOOD RECEIPTS FROM THE CHICKEN YARD

Back in the "good ole days", before the advent of air conditioned chicken houses and automated chicken feeders; it was a familiar sight. . .that of the little "hen house" (size depended on number of chickens, of course) and a fenced-in yard close by the family home. And it was an assigned job for some member of the family, every day to "feed the chickens". That member could be seen with his or her pan of chicken feed "cluckin'" the chickens to come eat as they strewed the feed in the yard. And coming for their part of the feed, the ducks sometimes scootin under the fence from their pond nearby. And the turkeys, ready to "gobble" anything and everything in sight. Gathering eggs from the hen house was another assigned chore for the boys and girls in the family. Eggs were carefully gathered and placed in the hand woven egg basket (a collectors item these days!), ready to "carry to town" to sell, sometimes door to door to regular "egg customers."

The chicken yard. . .a bit of Americana from yesteryear. Though you may never have had the experience of gathering eggs from the hen house, you can have the delightful experience of trying some of our "CACKLIN GOOD RECEIPTS FROM THE CHICKEN YARD", which we've gathered for your enjoyment.

To Fry Chickens

Cut up the chickens, and season them with salt and cayenne pepper; roll them in flour, and fry them in hot lard; when the whole are fried, pour off the lard, and put in a quarter of a pound of butter, one teacup of cream, a little flour, and some scalded parsley chopped fine, for the sauce.

This receipt has been around a long time. It was first printed in Godey's Lady's Book in 1861. Here's another place to use your heavy cast-iron skillet. Stay with it while you're cooking the chicken. Turn often.

Can't beat this one for. . . .

SOUTHERN-STYLE FRIED CHICKEN

2 2½-3 lb. broiler-fryer chickens, cut up
2 cups all-purpose flour
2 cups buttermilk
cooking oil

Season chicken with salt and pepper. Coat with some of the flour then dip into buttermilk; coat again with remaining flour. Pour oil into deep skillet and heat to 350°F. Regulate heat so chicken fries at 325°F. (if you have an electric skillet, otherwise take this hint from the pioneer cooks. . . . to test oil to see if it is hot enough to fry, sprinkle a small pinch of flour in oil, if it sizzles, it is hot enough, if it does not sizzle, let oil heat longer.) Fry a few pieces at a time, in hot oil 'til tender. . . . 12 to 15 minutes; turn once. Drain well. Serve hot or chilled. Makes 8 servings.

Another good old fashioned recipe is. . . .

OVEN FRIED CHICKEN

¾ cup melted butter or margarine
½ teaspoon salt
½ teaspoon seasoning salt
¼ teaspoon black pepper
1 2½-3 lb. broiler-fryer chicken, cut up
1 cup crushed cornflakes or crushed potato chips or ½ cup fine dry bread crumbs

Wash and dry chicken; sprinkle lightly with salt. Combine butter, salt, pepper, and seasoning salt. Brush chicken with butter mixture, then roll in cornflakes, potato chips or bread crumbs. Place chicken, skin side up, without touching in ungreased, large shallow baking pan. Bake at 375°F. 'til tender, about 1 hour. Do not turn. Serves 4.

BARBECUE FRIED CHICKEN

1 2½-3 lb. broiler-fryer chicken, cut up
¼ cup all-purpose flour
1 teaspoon salt
2 tablespoons cooking oil
1 cup catsup
½ cup chopped onion
½ cup water
1 small clove garlic, minced
1 teaspoon salt
¼ teaspoon pepper
3 tablespoons lemon juice

Coat chicken pieces with a mixture of the flour and the 1 teaspoon salt. In a 12-inch skillet, brown chicken in hot oil over medium heat about 15 minutes, turning to brown evenly. Meanwhile, in saucepan, combine catsup, onion, water, garlic, 1 teaspoon salt, and pepper. Bring to boiling. Simmer, uncovered, for 20 minutes. Remove from heat; blend in lemon juice. Add catsup mixture to chicken. Cover; cook over low heat until tender, 35 to 40 minutes; turn occasionally. Makes 4 servings.

Note: This recipe may be used with a Brown-In-Bag. Coat chicken and lay in bag in baking dish. Mix sauce and pour over chicken. Close bag with twist tie. . . . punch 6 to 8 holes into top of bag and cook 50 to 60 minutes at 375°F.

BARBECUE CHICKEN FAMILY STYLE

3-3½ lbs. frying chicken legs and breasts
salt and pepper
1 (8 oz.) can tomato sauce
2 tablespoons molasses
1 tablespoon prepared mustard
⅛ teaspoon liquid smoke
1 (53 oz.) can pork and beans
1 (12 oz.) can whole kernel corn with red & green sweet peppers, drained
3 tablespoons diced green chilies canned
1 (8½ oz.) package corn muffin mix

Arrange chicken pieces in single layer in 14" x 11½" x 2¼" open roaster; sprinkle with salt and pepper. Bake, uncovered, at 425°F. 30 minutes; drain excess fat. Meanwhile, combine tomato sauce, molasses, mustard, and liquid smoke. Use **half** to brush on partially cooked chicken; arrange in double layer in center of dish. Spoon pork and beans mixed with corn and green chilies on both sides of chicken. Bake, uncovered, 15 minutes. Prepare muffin mix according to package directions. Drop by spoonfuls over beans. Pour remaining sauce over chicken. Bake 15 to 20 minutes longer. Makes 8 to 10 servings.

SWEET N' SMOKEY OVEN BARBECUED CHICKEN

1 broiler-fryer chicken,
  cut up
½ cup water
1 large onion, sliced
1 teaspoon hickory smoked salt
¼ teaspoon pepper
2 tablespoons prepared mustard
½ cup catsup (hot)
½ cup cooking oil
½ cup maple syrup
¼ cup vinegar

In large shallow baking pan, place chicken, skin side up, in single layer. Pour water around chicken. Tuck onion slices in and around chicken. Sprinkle hickory smoked salt and pepper on chicken. Bake, uncovered, in 375°F. oven 30 minutes. In bowl, mix together, stirring constantly, mustard, catsup, oil, maple syrup, and vinegar. Pour over chicken and bake, uncovered, about 30 minutes or until fork can be inserted in chicken with ease. Makes 4 servings.

From California and the apricot growers. . . . comes this excellent recipe for. . . .

BARBECUED CHICKEN WINGS

1 can (17 oz.) apricot halves,
  drained
2 tablespoons catsup
2 tablespoons salad oil
1 tablespoon lemon juice
½ teaspoon salt
½ teaspoon liquid smoke (optional)
3 lbs. chicken wings (use the
  "drumstick" part, or whole
  wing, if desired)

Combine apricots, catsup, oil, lemon juice, salt and liquid smoke in electric blender. Blend until smooth. Place chicken wings on rack in shallow baking pan; brush with apricot sauce. Bake in 425°F. oven about 30 minutes, basting with sauce every 15 minutes. Serve extra sauce with chicken wings. Serves 6.

CHICKEN IMPERIAL

4 chicken breasts, cut in halves
1½ teaspoons salt
¼ cup margarine
⅓ cup dry sherry
2 teaspoon Worcestershire sauce
1 teaspoon curry powder
1 teaspoon dried leaf oregano
½ teaspoon dry mustard
½ teaspoon garlic powder
¼ teaspoon paprika
⅛ teaspoon Tabasco sauce

Sprinkle chicken breasts on both sides with salt. Place in large shallow baking pan. Combine remaining ingredients in small saucepan; stir over medium heat until margarine melts and mixture is smooth. Remove from heat; brush generously over chicken. Bake chicken in 350°F. oven 1-1½ hours or until tender, basting and turning chicken every 10 to 15 minutes. Serve garnished with spiced peaches and parsley. Makes 4 servings.

Friends from Sunkist Kitchens share this with us:

"IT'S AT HONEY" BAKED CHICKEN

2 broiler-fryers (3 lbs. each), cut into quarters
2 teaspoons grated orange peel
1 teaspoon grated lemon peel
1 cup freshly squeezed orange juice
1/3 cup freshly squeezed lemon juice
1/2 cup honey
2 tablespoons Worcestershire sauce
2 cloves garlic, crushed or finely minced
1 teaspoon dry mustard
1 teaspoon salt
salad oil

Place chicken quarters in glass dish. Combine remaining ingredients except salad oil; pour over chicken and marinate for 2 hours, turning every 30 minutes. Remove chicken; wipe partially dry with paper towel. Reserve marinade. Place chicken skin side down in shallow baking dish; brush lightly with salad oil. Bake at 375°F. for 35 minutes. Turn and bake 25 minutes longer, or until done. Meanwhile, boil reserved marinade, uncovered, until reduced to 3/4 cup, about 10 minutes. Glaze chicken with marinade and return to 450°F. oven for 2-3 minutes.

TARRAGON CHICKEN

Split in half 3 broiler chickens and arrange them, skin side up, in a broiling pan or tray. Sprinkle the chickens with salt and a generous amount of freshly ground black pepper. Melt 1/2 cup sweet butter and stir in 2 tablespoons tarragon vinegar and 1/4 teaspoon sugar. Spread the chickens generouly with the butter mixture and broil them, basting them frequently, until the skin is crisp and brown. When the butter mixture is all used, remove the chickens from the broiler, sprinkle them lavishly with chopped parsley and add 2 tablespoons water to the pan. Bake the chickens in a moderate (350°F.) oven for about 30 minutes, or until they are just tender. Serve with tomato preserves.

Tomato Preserves:
Peel 6 ripe tomatoes and chop them coarsely. Measure the tomatoes by cupfuls into a heavy saucepan and stir in an equal amount of sugar and 1/4 teaspoon salt. Cook the mixture over low heat, stirring frequently until it turns dark red in color and begins to thicken. Serve hot or cold.

Here is a mighty tasty low calorie recipe for. . . .

CHICKEN IN THE OVEN

3 broiler-fryer chickens, halved
3 teaspoons salt
1/2 teaspoon Tabasco
1 teaspoon paprika
4 tablespoons lime juice
2 tablespoons salad oil
2 teaspoons dried tarragon

Place chicken halves, skin side down, in shallow foil-lined baking pan. Combine remaining ingredients to make a marinade; brush over chickens. Bake in a 375°F. oven 45 to 50 minutes, turning over after first 25 minutes and brushing occasionally with marinade. Makes 6 servings.

CHICKEN AND DUMPLINGS

4-5 lb. stewing chicken
1/2 teaspoon ground sage (optional)
1 cup all-purpose flour
2 teaspoons baking powder
1/2 teaspoon salt
2 tablespoons snipped parsley
1 egg
1/4 cup milk
2 tablespoons butter, melted
1 cup cold water
1/2 cup all-purpose flour
1 1/2 teaspoons salt
1/8 teaspoon pepper

Prepare stewed chicken except add sage to cooking liquid, if desired.
Prepare dumplings when chicken is almost tender: stir together 1 cup flour, baking powder and 1/2 teaspoon salt; add parsley. Stir together egg, milk and melted butter. Add to flour mixture, stirring just till blended. Drop dough from tablespoon directly onto chicken in boiling broth. Cover tightly; return to boiling. Reduce heat; **do not lift cover.** Simmer 12-15 minutes. Remove dumplings and chicken to platter. Keep warm. Strain broth.

Thicken broth for gravy: In saucepan, bring 4 cups broth to boiling. Stir cold water into 1/2 cup flour; gradually add to broth, mixing well. Cook and stir till thickened and bubbly. Season with 1 1/2 teaspoons salt and pepper. Pour over chicken and dumplings. Serves 6 to 8.

CURRIED CHICKEN

1 frying-size chicken (2½-3 lbs.)
    cut in serving pieces
flour
½ teaspoon salt
¼ teaspoon pepper
dash paprika
shortening
1 medium onion, chopped
½ cup minced celery
1 medium apple, chopped
¼ cup pan drippings
¼ cup melted butter
2 tablespoons flour
1-2 tablespoons curry powder
1½ cups chicken stock

Roll each piece of chicken in flour seasoned with salt, pepper, and paprika. Cook in hot shortening until golden brown, remove from pan as it browns. Mix the onion, celery, and apple with the pan drippings and butter. Cook until light brown and add the 2 tablespoons flour, curry powder, and cook for a minute. Add the chicken stock. Check seasoning and adjust. Cook until thick. Replace chicken and simmer until tender . . . . about 30-40 minutes. Cook covered. Serve with plain boiled rice. Serves 6.

CHICKEN AND HAM CROQUETTES

2 eggs, beaten
2 tablespoons butter or margarine,
    melted
¾ cup soft bread crumbs (1 slice)
½ teaspoon dry mustard
dash ground nutmeg
dash pepper
3 cups ground cooked chicken or
    turkey
1 cup fully cooked ham, ground
1 beaten egg
½ cup fine dry bread crumbs
fat for frying
Caper Sauce

In mixing bowl combine the 2 beaten eggs, butter, soft bread crumbs, mustard, nutmeg, and pepper. Add chicken and ham, mix well. Chill. Shape cold chicken mixture into 12 logs . . . . using about ¼ cup mixture for each. Dip log in the remaining beaten egg, then roll in fine dry bread crumbs. Fry in deep hot oil (365°F.) for 2½-3 minutes. Drain well. Serve with Caper Sauce. Makes 6 servings.
Caper Sauce:
In small saucepan, melt 2 tablespoons butter or margarine; blend in 2 tablespoons all-purpose flour. Stir in ½ cup milk and ½ cup chicken broth; cook and stir until bubbly. Stir in 1 tablespoon capers.

CHICKEN PIE

4 lb. stewing chicken, cut in
pieces
4 sprigs of parsley
1 stalk celery, cut in large
pieces
1 bay leaf
1 onion stuck with 2 cloves
water (enough to barely cover
chicken)
1 cup diced potatoes
2-3 carrots
1 cup peas
12 small white onions
2 tablespoons butter
1 tablespoon flour
½ cup cream
2 cups chicken stock
salt and pepper to taste

In a kettle, put chicken, parsley, celery, bay leaf, onion stuck with cloves, and just enough water to barely cover chicken. Bring the liquid to a boil and simmer the chicken until it is tender when tested with a fork. Let chicken stand in the stock until it is cool enough to handle. Remove the chicken and strain the stock and reserve it. Discard skin and bones from the chicken and cut the meat into pieces. Cook separately in a little salted boiling water, the potatoes, carrots, peas and onions until the vegetables are tender. Drain them thoroughly. In a saucepan, melt the butter, stir in 1 tablespoon flour smoothly, and cook over low heat until it bubbles. Pour in the 2 cups of reserved chicken stock and ½ cup cream. Add salt and pepper to taste and cook the sauce, stirring constantly, until it is smooth and slightly thick. Combine the chicken, vegetables, and sauce in a deep glass pie dish. Cover the top of the dish with pastry, pressing the edges together securely. Bake the pie in a hot (425°F.) oven for 10 minutes, reduce heat to 350°F. and bake for 25-30 minutes longer.

Here's a different kind of pastry for your chicken pie. . . .

CHEDDAR CHEESE PASTRY
In a bowl work together ½ cup soft butter and 2 cups grated Cheddar cheese, at room temperature, until the mixture is creamy. Add 2 cups sifted flour sifted with ¼ teaspoon each: baking powder, dry mustard and paprika, and blend the pastry with the hands until it clings together.

No collection of chicken recipes would be complete without the original recipe for Country Captain. . . . which was created by the late Mrs. W. L. Bullard, a famous Columbus, Georgia hostess. She created it to serve at a special party for President Franklin D. Roosevelt and his distinguished guests at Warm Springs, Georgia.

COUNTRY CAPTAIN

3½-4 lb. young, tender hen
    (we now use breast only)
flour, salt, pepper
lard
2 onions, finely chopped
2 green peppers, chopped
1 small garlic bean, minced
1½ teaspoons salt
½ teaspoon white pepper
3 teaspoons curry powder
2 no.2 cans tomatoes
½ teaspoon chopped parsley
½ teaspoon powdered thyme
¼ lbs. almonds, scalded,
    skinned, roasted until
    golden brown
3 heaping tablespoons currants
2 cups cooked rice
parsley for garnish

Disjoint chicken for frying, or if using breast only. . . . remove skin and roll pieces in flour, salt and pepper. Brown in lard. Remove chicken from pan but keep it hot. (This is the secret to the dish's success. . . . .) Into the lard in which the chicken has been browned, put the onions, peppers and garlic. Cook very slowly, stirring constantly. Season with salt, pepper and curry powder. (Test curry to suit your own taste.) Add tomatoes, parsley and thyme. Put chicken in roaster and pour mixture over it. If it does not cover the chicken, add water to skillet in which mixture has been cooked and pour over chicken, also. Cover roaster tightly. Bake in moderate oven about 45 minutes. . . until the chicken is tender. Place chicken in center of a large platter and pile the rice around it, cooked very dry with every grain standing alone. Now, drop currants into sauce mixture and pour over rice. Scatter almonds on top. Garnish with parsley, and you have "food for the gods."

CHICKEN CROQUETTE FROM THE OVEN

2 tablespoons butter or margarine
3 tablespoon all-purpose flour
½ cup milk
½ cup chicken broth
2 cups ground or finely chopped
    cooked chicken or turkey
1 tablespoon snipped parsley
¼ teaspoon salt
⅛ teaspoon dried sweet basil,
    crushed
8 slices white bread
2 beaten eggs
2 tablespoons butter, melted
Cranberry-Claret Sauce

Melt the 2 tablespoons butter; blend in flour. Add milk and broth cook and stir till bubbly. Cool slightly. Add chicken, parsley, salt, beaten eggs and basil. Cover; chill several hours. Trim crusts from bread; cutbread in ½-inch cubes. Shape chicken mixture into 8 balls, then coat with bread cubes. Place in greased shallow baking pan. Brush with 2 tablespoons melted butter. Bake at 375°F. till hot and toasted, about 30 minutes. Serve with sauce. Makes 4 servings.

CRANBERRY-CLARET SAUCE

Heat together 1 8-oz. jar jellied cranberry sauce and ¼ cup Claret. Beat till mixture is smooth.

Cooked chicken in a creamy marinade layered with Ritz crackers..

QUICK 'N EASY CHICKEN CASSEROLE

¾ cup mayonnaise
¾ cup dairy sour cream·
¼ cup India relish
2 tablespoons finely chopped
    onion
1 teaspoon salt
1 cup milk
1 (4 oz.) jar whole pimientos,
    drained, cut in pieces
3 cups cooked chicken, cut in
    chunks (about 1 lb.)
54 Ritz crackers, finely rolled
    (about 2¼ cups crumbs)
1 tablespoon butter or marga-
    rine, melted

Combine first 6 ingredients. Stir in next 2 ingredients. Sprinkle ¾ cup crumbs over bottom of 12" x 8" x8" baking dish. Cover with half of chicken mixture. Repeat layers. Mix butter with remaining crumbs. Sprinkle evenly over top. Bake in a preheated moderate oven (350°F.) about 20 minutes, or until heated through. Makes about 6 (8 oz.) servings. Serve with wedges of lettuce, your favorite dressing and fresh apples for dessert.

Oranges taste great with salad dressing of all types and add the extra color and flavor that tossed salads need. Here's a salad that gets its flavor and color boost from oranges. Try it!

A NEW CHICKEN SALAD

1 tablespoon fresh grated orange
  peel
2 oranges, peeled, cut into bite-
  size pieces
1½ cups chopped cooked chicken
⅔ cup chopped celery
½ cup sliced toasted almonds
1 package (3 oz.) cream cheese,
  softened
2-3 tablespoons mayonnaise or
  salad dressing
½ teaspoon salt
⅛ teaspoon pepper
Lettuce cups

Combine all ingredients except lettuce. Spoon about 1 cup chicken mixture into each lettuce cup. Makes 4 servings. (May also be used as sandwich filling.)

CHICKEN SALAD

3-4 cups chopped, cooked
  chicken
2 cups chopped celery
1 cup chopped sweet cucumber pickles, or as desired
5-6 finely chopped hard-
  cooked eggs
1 cup pineapple chunks (save
  part of juice to mix with
  mayonnaise)
½ cup chopped English
  walnuts
1 tablespoon lemon juice
½ teaspoon salt, or to taste
dash red pepper
½ cup mayonnaise

Place chicken in large bowl and add celery, pickles, pineapple, walnuts and eggs. Season with lemon juice, salt and red pepper. Mix mayonnaise with a little of the pineapple juice and mix thoroughly with chicken mixture. Serves 12 to 14.

If you like a hot taste to your chicken salad, you'll like this one. . . .

CHICKEN SALAD WITH A ZING

½ cup mayonnaise
1 cup sour cream
½ teaspoon Tabasco
¾ teaspoon curry powder
½ teaspoon salt
2 tablespoons lime or lemon
   juice
2 teaspoons grated onion
1 tablespoon caper, optional
3 cups diced cooked chicken
1 cup diced celery

Blend together mayonnaise, sour cream, Tabasco, curry powder, salt, lime or lemon juice, onion and capers. Combine chicken and celery in a large bowl; add dressing and toss lightly. Refrigerate several hours before serving. Makes 4 servings.

EASY TURKEY CASSEROLE

2 can (10½ oz. each) condensed
   cream of celery soup
¾ cup milk
1½ cups cooked vegetables
3 cups cooked turkey, cut up
2 cups Bisquick baking mix
½ cup cold water
½ cup cranberry sauce

Heat soup and milk, stirring frequently. Stir in vegetables and turkey; heat through. Pour mixture into ungreased 3-quart casserole. Keep hot while preparing topping. Stir baking mix and water to a soft dough. Gently smooth dough into a ball on floured cloth-covered board. Knead 5 times. Roll dough into a rectangle 12 x 9 inches; spread with cranberry sauce. Roll up, beginning at wide side; cut into 1-inch slices. Place slices cut side down on hot turkey mixture. Bake uncovered 20 minutes or until biscuits are golden brown. Serves 6 to 8.

Never tried batter fried turkey 'til we found this recipe:

BATTER FRIED TURKEY

8-10 pieces of left over turkey
   (breast, thigh or pieces of leg)
1 cup turkey broth
1½ cups flour
add salt, pepper and paprika
   to taste

Have turkey cut into serving pieces. Combine all above ingredients for batter. Mix well. Dip turkey pieces in batter and fry in deep fat until golden brown.

You may want to serve this with sweet and sour sauce or with gravy made with more broth as you would make any white gravy.

Here's a good thing to do with left over turkey....

TURKEY POT PIE

Filling:
¼ cup chopped onion
¼ cup butter or margarine
⅓ cup Bisquick baking mix
1 teaspoon salt
½ teaspoon pepper
⅔ cup light cream
2 cups chicken broth*
3-4 cups cut-up cooked turkey
1 tablespoon chopped pimiento
1 teaspoon Worcestershire
    sauce

Cook and stir onion in butter in large saucepan until tender. Blend in baking mix, salt and pepper. Cook over low heat, stirring until mixture is bubbly. Remove from heat. Stir in remaining ingredients. Heat to boiling, stirring constantly. Boil and stir one minute. Pour into ungreased baking dish. Keep hot. Top with your favorite canned biscuits or your favorite biscuit recipe....or pat or roll pie crust dough into a rectangle, 11 x 7. Cut 2 or 3 slits in center and place over hot filling. Bake about 15 minutes. Serves 4 to 6.

*Chicken broth can be used by dissolving 2 chicken bouillon cubes in 2 cups boiling water, or use canned chicken broth.

Another idea for left over turkey....have no idea who created it but it is a really delicious casserole....and called simply:

TURKEY CASSEROLE

2 cups sliced cooked turkey
2 cups cooked asparagus
2 cups turkey or chicken broth
    (seasoned to taste)
6 tablespoons flour
½ teaspoon salt
⅓ cup melted butter
2½ cups cream (or milk if you
    prefer a less rich dish)
1½ cups pre-cooked rice (cook
    with salt to taste)
¾ cup grated sharp cheese
3 tablespoons toasted slivered
    almonds
⅓ cup finely chopped onion

Make sauce with flour, salt and the melted butter. Add cream, or milk and stir over moderate heat until thickened.
Place cooked rice in 2 quart baking dish. Pour broth over rice. Sprinkle half the cheese and the onion over rice....top with the asparagus and then the turkey. Pour sauce over casserole and sprinkle with remaining cheese. Bake in 350°F oven for 25-30 minutes, remove from oven and sprinkle with the toasted almonds. Serves 6-8.

Vegetables from the Garden and Fruits from the Orchard

VEGETABLES FROM THE GARDEN AND
FRUITS FROM THE ORCHARD

Vegetables create quite a picture in "Mr. Cason's Vegetable Garden" and we're sure he'd pass along some of these "things to look for" whether you're picking vegetables from your own garden or from the grocery.

Beans or peas: Snap or yellow beans should be crisp and tender and filled with only small seed, if you want them to really taste good. Lima beans should be fresh, dark green and well filled with plump seed. Pea pods should be light green in color and filled with well developed peas. Both beans and peas should be used immediately after they're picked, their flavor and quality fade quickly.

Cabbage: Best heads should be firm and "heavy" feeling and have a bright, light green color.

Corn: Husks should be fresh-looking green and still moist enough to fit firmly around the cob. Milky, well developed kernels are notes of good corn.

Cucumbers: Pick them when tiny or medium size with a shiny, bright green color.

Potatoes: The best are firm, fairly smooth and free from "eyes". If you're digging, try not to bruise or cut; "new" potatoes bruise easily and do not keep as well as "late" potatoes.

Squash: More varieties than you can shake a stick at! But generally divided into two kinds:
　　Summer Squash: includes zucchini and white bush scallop
　　Winter Squash: favorite kinds, butternut and acorn
Pick when a little immature, but if you're "picking" in the grocery or roadside stand, avoid the ones with soft or discolored spots.

Tomatoes: (Did you know that the tomato is technically a fruit, but grown and sold as a vegetable?) The best ones are vine ripened. . .nothing better! But for shipping purposes the grower picks them when just turning red. You still want to pick them with a good color and skins free from cracks or scars. Do not ripen in the sun, pick a spot away from the window and let ripen at room temperature.

Onions: Garden green onions are at their best when the tops are just about 3 or 4 inches above the root. Same goes for scallions or leeks, store in refrigerator vegetable bin.

From the Orchard

Apples: You know that delicious, red or golden (McIntosh and Jonathan) are the best. And if you're wanting them for cooking, Rome Beauty, Northern Spy are best favorites with us.

Peaches: That pretty red blush doesn't always indicate a good peach. The best ones are firm, but not really hard and are a rich creamy or yellow color. In Georgia, the "Peach State" you can take your "pick" of a half dozen really top varieties.

Grapes: Pick them when they're fresh looking and firmly attached to the stems. Check them by gently shaking the bunch. A few, if any should fall off.

Pears: Pick a pear before it's ripe and let it mellow in a cool place in the house. Russeting or brown roughening does not affect the taste.

Back in the "good ole' days" most vegetables were either served raw, boiled, baked or fried. Seasonings included salt, pepper and a little grease, salt pork or butter. Sometimes when "company was comin' " . . . . they could be enhanced with sauces and cooked in casseroles called "baked puddings". For instance the lowly turnip became a

COMPANY TURNIP CASSEROLE

6 or 8 good size turnips
1 teaspoon salt
2 teaspoons sugar
1 cup white sauce (today we might use a can of celery soup undiluted)
½ cup bread crumbs
4 tablespoons butter (melted)

Slice and boil turnips in salt water to taste. Cook until tender. Drain and arrange in a baking dish. Sprinkle with the salt and sugar. Add sauce or soup. Top with bread crumbs and pour melted butter over. Bake at 350°F. for about 30 minutes. Could become a favorite dish!

When tomatoes, corn, okra and onions are plentiful. . . . here's a dish you'll want to cook over and over. . . . just right for a country dinner!

VEGETABLE CASSEROLE

4 cups fresh corn, (cut and scraped from cob, about 8 medium ears)
1 cup fresh okra, sliced
1 cup soft bread crumbs
⅓ cup onion, finely chopped
3 teaspoons salt
½ teaspoon black pepper
2 teaspoons sugar
⅓ cup butter
2 cups milk
4 eggs, beaten
3 fresh tomatoes
3 additional tablespoons butter, melted
salt and pepper to sprinkle over tomatoes

Preheat oven to 350°F. Combine corn, okra, bread crumbs, onions, salt, pepper and sugar. Melt butter in saucepan and add milk. Stir vegetable mixture and milk mixture together. Cook over low heat about five minutes or until thickened. . . . remove from heat. Add a little to the mixture into the eggs. Then add to the remaining mixture. (Do a little at a time so eggs will not cook in the hot mixture!) Pour into buttered 2 quart casserole and bake one hour or until firm. Cut tomatoes into ½ inch slices and arrange over top of casserole about 15 minutes before end of baking time. Brush tomatoes with melted butter, sprinkle with salt and pepper lightly (may want to use just a touch of oregano also!). Tomatoes will be just slightly cooked. Serve hot. . . . and often!

Don't know if Grandmother ever thought about marinating vegetables or not. . . . but she really missed a good one. . . . if she never tried this idea:

MARINATED VEGETABLES

1 can green beans
1 can green peas
1 can whole kernel corn
1 can chopped pimentos
1 can water chestnuts
1 small jar stuffed olives
1 cup cauliflower, pulled in small
    pieces from the stem
2 onions, sliced
1 cup carrots, slightly cooked
Marinade:
1 cup sugar
¾ cup salad oil (vegetable oil)
1 cup vinegar
1 teaspoon Tabasco
1 teaspoon salt
1 teaspoon pepper

Take first six ingredients from the pantry shelf. Drain, and add cauliflower, onions and carrots. Drain vegetables and heat ingredients for the marinade. Add the vegetables and marinate for several hours or overnight. Absolutely "crunchy" good!

Found this recipe in an old magazine. . . . reminiscent of Mama's green fried tomatoes. . . . try it with either green or ripe tomatoes!

SAUTEED TOMATOES

4 large tomatoes
2 eggs
½ cup milk
2 tablespoons vegetable oil
½ teaspoon garlic salt
1 cup flour
2 cups dry bread crumbs
½ cup additional vegetable oil
½ cup butter or oleo
½ cup finely chopped parsley
salt

Cut tomatoes in ¼ inch slices. Let stand while you beat eggs, milk, 2 tablespoons oil and garlic salt. Wipe the tomatoes with paper towels. Dip each slice in flour and then into egg mixture. . . . then dip in bread crumbs. Let stand a few minutes. Put ½ the remaining oil in skillet over medium heat. Add one half the butter. Saute (lightly brown) tomatoes on each side. Remove to warm platter and proceed with the remaining tomatoes. . . . using the remaining butter and oil. Sprinkle with the finely chopped parsley and serve. Should be servings for 8.

Fresh corn....so many things to be said for it....you can fry it, boil it....souffle it....but you'll never forget the taste of it....in Grandmother's fresh corn casserole or pudding!

CORN PUDDING

2 cups fresh corn cut from the cob (cut and scrape cob, do not cut whole kernels!)
3 eggs
¼ cup flour
1 teaspoon salt
½ teaspoon pepper
1 tablespoon sugar
2 cups cream
2 tablespoons melted butter

Beat eggs thoroughly....mix flour, salt, pepper, sugar, butter and stir into eggs. Stir in the corn and cream. Pour into lightly greased baking dish (1½ quart size)....place in a pan of hot water and bake in a moderate (325°F.) oven for 1 hour or until knife inserted in center comes out dry.

OLD FASHIONED STEWED CORN
(none better!)

8-10 ears fresh corn
1½ cups water
3 tablespoons butter
2 tablespoons sugar
salt and pepper to taste
bacon drippings

Melt butter with about two tablespoons bacon drippings. Mix corn with water and sugar, salt and pepper. Bring to a boil stirring constantly. Turn heat down to medium heat and continue cooking and stirring often until corn is tender. (May have to add a little more water as corn cooks.) Watch carefully to prevent sticking or burning.

Garden peas!....As Country as Country itself....and you just can't beat....

COUNTRY STYLE PEAS WITH BACON

½ pound bacon
2 cups finely chopped onion
2 pounds fresh peas (cooked and drained)
½ teaspoon sugar
2 tablespoons chopped parsley

Cook bacon until crisp and remove from fat. Remove all fat from pan except two tablespoons....to this add the onion and cook until tender. Add peas, bacon (which you have crumbled) and the sugar. Mix well and heat thoroughly. Sprinkle with the parsley and serve! Serves from four to six.

Nobody. . . . could cook beans with the taste like. . . .

MAMA'S OLD SOUTH GREEN BEANS

3 lbs. fresh green beans
1 piece of streaked meat (maybe
about ¼ lb.)
salt to taste
dash of black pepper

String the beans. Break into two inch pieces. Scald and pour water off. Place in heavy kettle (heavy aluminum. . . . but heavy stainless steel or a cast iron kettle is best.) Cover with water 2" above beans. Bring to a boil and turn heat down to medium. . . . cook for fifteen minutes and then add meat, salt and pepper. Bring to boil and then turn to medium low heat. . . . cook until meat is tender (till its ready to fall apart). . . . beans are very tender. . . . all the juice is gone to the point where they're almost ready to stick to kettle. . . . serve with cornbread, corn, okra and buttermilk! Real south eatin'. . . . Note: Scrape skin off meat and slice in thin slices down to the skin but not through skin. . . . makes it cook faster. . . .

Everybody has their favorite green bean casserole. . . . hope this one becomes a fovorite with you. . . . not fancy. . . . just good!

GREEN BEAN CASSEROLE

2 no.303 cans cut green beans
1 cup chopped onion (use a little
green onion with tops too)
¼ cup butter
4 tablespoons flour
1 small can/jar mushroom pieces
1½ cups milk
1 teaspoon soy sauce
½ teaspoon black pepper
salt to taste
½ pound Velveeta Cheese

Saute finely chopped onion in butter. . . . add flour and blend. Stir in milk and add other seasonings. Cook until it begins to thicken. Remove from fire and add cheese, stirring until melted. Add mushrooms with juice from can. Blend. Pour sauce over beans. Place in casserole and bake at 325°F. for about 40 minutes. Serves 8.

There's nothing quite as good as fried okra picked fresh from the garden . . . . coated with a corn-meal-flour mixture and fried to perfection! Try this:

FRIED OKRA

1 lb. fresh okra, washed and dried
½ cup flour
1 cup corn meal
¾ teaspoon salt
2 eggs
¼ cup milk
enough oil for frying

Trim ends from each piece of okra and cut into ½ inch slices. Set aside. Mix together flour, corn meal and salt. Beat eggs well and add milk. Mix well. Put about 1½ inches vegetable oil in skillet (if cast iron . . . . test by dropping piece okra in and if it sizzles . . . . OK!) If using electric skillet . . . . have temperature at 375⁰. With slotted spoon dip okra through the egg mixture and then roll in the corn meal and flour mixture. Coat well and put a few pieces at at time into the hot vegetable oil. Cook about five minutes (or until golden brown) turning occasionally. Drain on paper towels and serve while hot.

Good Suggestion: Double recipe . . . . it's **that** good!

BAKED CARROTS

1 bunch carrots (7-8 carrots)
¼ cup chopped onion
4 tablespoons butter
1 teaspoon lemon juice
1 teaspoon finely chopped crystallized ginger
3 tablespoons honey
½ teaspoon salt
½ cup water

Scrape carrots and shred. Heat oven to 400°F. Cook onion in the butter until tender. Mix onion with shredded carrots. Place in one quart casserole. Mix the water, lemon juice, ginger, honey and salt. Pour over carrots. Dot with another tablespoon butter. Cover and cook in oven until tender . . . . about 45-50 minutes.

PICKLED BLACKEYED PEAS

2 cans blackeyed peas
1 medium onion, sliced
1 bottle oil and vinegar dressing

Drain and rinse peas. Pour dressing over peas and onion and chill.

The lowly sweet potato takes on a new look (and taste) when prepared by the following recipe given to us by that lovely lady, best known as a "Patron of the Arts", Mrs. Simon Schwob. You'll love the delightfully different taste.

SWEET POTATO CASSEROLE

2 cans (1 lb. 13 oz. cans) sweet
  potatoes
6 oz. frozen orange juice concentrate
¼ cup Maple syrup
¼ cup brown sugar
2 tablespoons butter
½ teaspoon salt
¼ cup finely chopped crystalized
  ginger

Drain sweet potatoes and save liquid. Halve or quarter the potatoes to serving size pieces. Place liquid in saucepan and boil until about one half the amount. Add orange juice, syrup, brown sugar and ginger. Bring to a boil. Cook for about 1 minute. Melt butter in a skillet and add potatoes. Saute until all are browned. Place potatoes in a 4 cup casserole and sprinkle with salt. Pour the syrup over potatoes and bake in 350° oven for 45 minutes. If you like, sprinkle chopped pecans over potatoes before pouring the syrup over them. You may prepare this casserole the day before serving. Store in refrigerator and heat thoroughly before serving.

TURNIP GREENS

8 cups turnip greens
½ pound salt pork or bacon
1 medium onion, chopped
1 cup diced turnips (root section)
salt and pepper to taste
1 cup water

Wash the greens, over and over again to remove any grit. Prepare 8 cups greens, and as you wash, remove stems. Place greens in heavy kettle. Add pork or bacon, onions, turnips, seasonings and water. Cover tightly and cook, on medium low heat, until meat is done. Greens will be delicious.

FRIED CABBAGE

3 tablespoons butter or margarine
5 cups coarsely chopped cabbage
1 medium chopped onion
1 teaspoon salt
dash nutmeg
½ tablespoon sugar
2 tablespoons vinegar
cayenne pepper

Melt butter in a deep sauce pan over low heat. Add cabbage, onion, salt, and nutmeg. Cover and cook slowly, stirring often (20 minutes). Do not brown. Add the sugar and cayenne to the vinegar. Mix. Pour over cabbage, cover, and cook 5 minutes more. One peeled, cored and chopped tart apple may be cooked with the cabbage, if desired. Serves 2-3.

Folks seen to enjoy sharing their "hand me down" recipes and Joreka Loomis, for many years Home Economist with General Electric. . . . says this is one she's happy to "hand down". . . .

MINTED GLAZED CARROTS

8 carrots
¼ cup orange juice
1 tablespoon chopped fresh mint
¼ cup water
2 tablespoons butter

Wash and scrape carrots. Cut into long strips. Arrange in oven casserole dish. Put water, orange juice and butter over carrots. Cover and bake in 350°F. oven for 50 minutes. When ready to serve, sprinkle with finely chopped mint.

Joreka also says. . . . it's "right handy" (if you don't have room for a garden or herb bed). . . . to grow mint in a hanging basket right in the kitchen window or from the back porch rafter.

Sweet and Sour Onions. . . . as suggested by Donna Downen, University of Georgia Extension Service. . . . maybe you hadn't thought that onions could make such a good casserole dish. . . . and Vidalia Onions (grown only in Vidalia, Georgia. . . . the true ones, that is) . . . . make this recipe even better than just an ordinary onion!

SWEET AND SOUR ONIONS

4 very large onions, peeled
¼ cup cider vinegar
¼ cup melted butter
¼ cup boiling water
¼ cup sugar

Slice the onions about ¼ inch thick. . . . arrange in a one quart baking dish. Mix all the other ingredients and pour over the onions. Bake in a preheated 300°F. oven for 1 hour. Serves 4 to 6.

This recipe was given to Anna Moore by Mrs. Uhla Leger, of Cordele, GA. A very unusual way for cooking sweet potatoes.

CANDIED SWEET POTATOES

4 fresh sweet potatoes (medium)
1 cup sugar mixed together with 1
   tablespoon flour
½ to 1 cup heavy cream
cinnamon
butter or margarine

Peel and dice sweet potatoes. Cook in salted, boiling water until just tender. Drain. Grease an 8"x8" baking dish. Layer half the potatoes in bottom of baking dish. Spoon half the flour-sugar mixture over potatoes. Sprinkle liberally with ground cinnamon (to taste) then dot with butter or margarine. Repeat with remaining potatoes, then the flour-sugar mixture, cinnamon and butter. Slowly pour heavy cream over potatoes until just barely covered. Bake in 350°F. oven for approximately 1 hour. Cream should be thick enough that it will not run when pan is tipped to one side. Serves 4.

You may use Half and Half or evaporated milk in place of heavy cream. However, the cream gives a better flavor.

SWEET POTATO CASSEROLE

6 to 8 medium sweet potatoes
1 stick butter
½ cup milk
⅓ cup apricot brandy
3 tablespoons molasses
⅓ cup sugar

Pare and slice sweet potatoes. Cook in boiling water until tender (very tender!). Drain well. Place potatoes in mixer or mash and beat well by hand. Add butter and sugar while hot and mix well. Add molasses and brandy. Grease casserole with butter and pour potato mixture into it. . . . sprinkle additional sugar over top. . . . may take an additional half cup or more. . . . (this will form a crust on top of potatoes). Bake uncovered in 350°F. oven for 25 to 30 minutes. This recipe can be frozen or made ahead and stored in refrigerator (when doing this leave off sugar until you bake).

Mighty good eatin'. . . .

EGGPLANT PARMESAN**

2 15oz. cans Hunt's tomato sauce
2 1½oz. envelopes dry spaghetti
   sauce mix
1 cup finely chopped onion
½ cup water
2 teaspoons seasoned salt
2 large eggplants, pared and sliced
   ½ inch thick
8 oz. Mozzarella cheese, shredded
⅓ cup grated Parmesan cheese

Combine first 5 ingredients in saucepan; blend well. Heat until boiling; simmer 5 minutes. In a 12¼"x10¼"x2¼" open roaster, arrange alternate layers of sauce mixture, eggplant and mozzarella starting with sauce mixture. Top with Parmesan cheese. Bake at 375°F. 35 to 40 minutes. Makes 10 to 12 servings.

**A quick and easy dish made with convenience foods. . . . canned sauce and sauce mix.

An unforgettable EGGPLANT CASSEROLE. . . .

2 medium size eggplant (how nice
   when fresh from the garden!)
½ teaspoon salt
1 cup flour
1 cup vegetable oil
1 tablespoon butter
¼ cup finely chopped green
   onion
4 cups canned tomatoes (coarsely
   chopped) or equal amount of
   fresh tomatoes, chopped
½ teaspoon celery salt
1 teaspoon sweet basil, crumbled
1 bay leaf
½ teaspoon sugar
1 teaspoon additional salt
¼ teaspoon coarse black pepper
¾ cup toasted (or packaged)
   bread crumbs
¾ cup parmesan cheese

Peel eggplant and cut in one inch cubes. Sprinkle with salt and let stand for about 30 minutes. Drain and dry with paper towels. Sprinkle with flour. . . . tossing lightly to cover all pieces. Heat half cup oil in large skillet (low heat) and add eggplant. Brown lightly on all sides and cook for 3 or 4 minutes. Remove from oil and set aside. Then cook the rest of eggplant cubes the same way in remaining oil. Melt the butter over medium heat and lightly brown the green onion and add the tomatoes, celery salt, basil, bay leaf, sugar, salt and pepper. Bring to boil and simmer for 10 minutes. Place eggplant in buttered 2 quart baking dish. Pour tomato mixture over and sprinkle with bread crumbs and cheese. Bake at 400°F. for 20-25 minutes.

Absolutely delicious!

BROCCOLI CASSEROLE

2 packages chopped broccoli
1 large onion
1 stick margarine
1 cup rice
2 cans cream of mushroom soup
1½ cups grated cheese, medium
   or sharp (save ½ cup of
   cheese to put on top)

Cook rice according to package directions. Cook broccoli, drain well. Saute onion in margarine and mix all ingredients together. Put in a buttered casserole 9"x11". This casserole may also be put in the freezer if you would like to make it up ahead of time. Take out and thaw at room temperature before baking. Bake at 375° 30-35 minutes.

BAKED ACORN SQUASH

2 medium acorn squash
1 teaspoon salt
¼ teaspoon pepper
4 teaspoons butter or margarine,
   softened
4 teaspoons brown sugar

Wash squash thoroughly. Cut in halves lenghtwise, and remove seeds and stringy portions. Place halves, cut side down, in shallow baking pan containing about ¼-inch of water. Bake at 400°F for 30 minutes. Turn cut side up, spread over each half, 1 teaspoon softened butter or margarine, and sprinkle with salt, pepper, and brown sugar. Bake at 400°F for about 30 minutes, or more until flesh is soft when tested with a fork. Note: This method may be used for baking large winter squash, but before baking, cut squash into serving size pieces.

Simply good....

BUTTERED SQUASH AND ONIONS

2 pounds squash
1 large onion
2 tablespoons butter
2 teaspoons sugar
⅓ cup water
salt and pepper to taste

Wash the squash (summer squash is best), cut into slices about ½-inch thick. Peel onions and cut them into slices about ¼-inch thick. Cook squash and onions together with the water, butter, salt, sugar and pepper. Cook until tender...about 15-20 minutes. Do not over cook. (However, some folks like to cook squash until soft enough to mash and continue cooking until thick.) Serves 4 to 5.

From up Virginia way comes another delicious squash recipe....

FRENCH FRIED SQUASH

4 medium summer squash, sliced
  thin
3 eggs
1 teaspoon salt
2 cups corn meal
½ cup milk
oil for frying

Beat eggs. Combine with milk and salt. Dip slices of squash into egg mixture. Roll in corn meal and fry in deep fat until tender. Serve hot.

BUTTERNUT SQUASH SOUFFLE

4 cups diced, peeled butternut
  squash
1 cup water
½ teaspoon salt
½ cup melted butter
1 cup brown sugar
½ teaspoon cinnamon
½ cup evaporated milk
1 cup marshmallows

Preheat oven to 350°F. Grease 1½ quart casserole. Put squash, water and salt in saucepan. Cover; bring to boil; cook for 15 minutes, or until tender. Drain; put in mixing bowl. Mash. Add remaining ingredients; mix well. Turn into casserole. Bake for 30 minutes.

LARRY'S STUFFED SQUASH

12 medium size yellow squash
2 10-oz. packages frozen chopped
　spinach
1 13-oz. package cream cheese,
　softened
3 eggs, well beaten
6 tablespoons melted margarine
1½ tablespoons sugar
½ teaspoon seasoned salt
½ teaspoon onion salt
1 tablespoon coarse ground black
　pepper
1 lb. bacon, cook and crumbled
1 cup butter cracker crumbs
paprika

Wash squash and drop into boiling water; cover and simmer for 8-10 minutes until tender but still firm. Drain and cool; cut stem end off and slice in half lenghtwise. Scoop out pulp; leaving firm shells. Mash pulp, cook spinach according to package directions, and drain well. Add squash pulp, cream cheese to spinach and mix well. Add next six ingredients and stir well. Spoon into shells. Sprinkle with cracker crumbs, paprika and bacon. Place in greased baking dish; cover with foil and bake at 325°F for 30 minutes. Serves 12.

Here's one even our great-grandmothers used. . . .

SKILLET SQUASH AND ONIONS

2 lbs. yellow summer squash
3 medium onions, sliced thin
3 tablespoons butter or margarine
½ teaspoon salt
¼ teaspoon pepper

Wash squash and dice. Combine all ingredients in skillet. Cover and cook for 20 to 30 minutes, or until squash and onions are tender, stirring frequently. Makes 4 servings.

GRITS AND CHEESE CASSEROLE

4 cups milk
*1 cup Speckled Heart grits
½ cup butter or margarine
2 eggs, well beaten
½ teaspoon baking powder
¼ teaspoon salt
1 cup grated Cheddar cheese

Preheat oven to 375°F. Bring 3½ cups milk to boiling point. Gradually stir in grits; cook over medium heat, stirring constantly, until thick, about 10 minutes. Remove from heat. Add butter; stir until melted. Stir in eggs, baking powder, salt and remaining milk. Pour into 2-quart caserole. Bake, uncovered 30 minutes. . . . then sprinkle grated cheese over top. Bake 15 minutes longer. Makes 6-8 servings.

*A good place to buy Speckled Heart Grits is Callaway Gardens Country Store.

BUTTERED HOMINY

2 #2½ cans whole hominy
3 tablespoons margarine or bacon
    fat
½ teaspoon paprika
salt

Heat the hominy in its own liquor. Drain, and then add seasonings. Hominy takes the place of potatoes.

Often I melt the fat, add the drained hominy, and saute until it is golden brown. Then season.

CLASSIC CHEESE LASAGNE

2 15-oz. cans Hunt's tomato herb
    sauce
1 cup minced onion
1 tablespoon seasoned salt
1½ teaspoons Italian herb
    seasoning
1 teaspoon garlic powder
3 eggs, beaten
1 16-oz. carton Ricotta cheese
1 8-oz. carton small curd cottage
    cheese
1 lb. lasagna noodles, cooked and
    drained
2 lbs. Mozzarella cheese, thinly
    sliced
½ cup grated Parmesan cheese

In bowl, combine tomato sauce, onion, seasoned salt, Italian seasoning, and garlic powder. Set aside. Blend eggs, Ricotta and cottage cheese in small bowl. Spoon a little sauce mixture into a 14"x11½"x2¼" baking dish to coat bottom; arrange layers of half each: cooked noodles, Ricotta mixture, sauce mixture and Mozzarella slices. Repeat layers; sprinkle with Parmesan. Bake at 375°F. 40-45 minutes. Let stand 10 minutes before cutting. Makes 10 to 12 servings.

Sweet Potato - Apple Casserole. . . . Must be good. . . . recommended by the people who grow them:

SWEET POTATO - APPLE CASSEROLE

3 large cooked sweet potatoes,
    sliced
4 tart apples
¼ cup sugar
½ teaspoon salt
1 tablespoon butter
¼ cup raisins

Wash and core and quarter apples. (Leave peelings on!) Place alternate layers of sweet potatoes and apples in greased baking dish. Sprinkle with sugar and salt and raisins. Repeat until all used. Dot the top layer of the casserole with butter. Add enough hot water (and some orange juice if available) just to cover bottom of dish. Cover and bake at 350°F, for 45 minutes or until apples are tender.

Grandma's old south brandied peaches. . . . a must when the peaches "come in". . . .

BRANDIED PEACHES

2 lbs. fresh whole peaches
1½ lbs. sugar
same amount of water as sugar
   (cup for cup)
¼ lb. baking soda
brandy

Put the soda in a large kettle of water and bring to a boil. (This is additional water to recipe a-bove. . . for preparing peaches only). When water is boiling, put peaches in a couple at a time so water will not stop boiling. Let them remain in this for about five minutes. Then place them in cold water and rub fuzz and skin off with a towel. . . . throwing them in cold water after each rubbing. Continue until all fruit is prepared. Make a syrup using the sugar and water (equal parts, remember) when it has been brought to a boil. Drop in peaches and cook until peaches can be easily pierced with a fork. Pack into hot sterilized jars. Fill with half syrup and half brandy. Great with all kinds of meats!

Another recipe from country New England. . . .

SPICED PEACHES

2 cups white sugar
3 cups brown sugar
2 cups vinegar
2 cinnamon sticks
2 tablespoons whole cloves
4 quarts peaches
1 tablespoon mustard seed
½ cup finely chopped crystalized
   ginger

Scald peaches in hot water. Re-move skins. Cook sugar, vinegar and spices for 20 minutes. Drop in peaches, a few at a time. Cook until tender. Pack in hot, sterilized jars. Add enough syrup to cover fruit. Seal. Makes 6 pints.

(You can cook seckel pears in this same way. . . . just wash and do not peel. Also leave stems on fruit.)

From Vermont's countryside comes this simple, simply delicious recipe for baked fresh peaches.

BAKED PEACHES

6 large fresh peaches
¾ cup maple syrup
dash freshly ground nutmeg
1 tablespoon finely chopped
   crystalized ginger

Butter a baking dish (large enough to give 12 peach halves room!). Peel peaches and cut in half. Remove pit. Place cut side down in buttered dish. Mix ginger with syrup and pour over peaches. Cook at 350°F, for about 25 minutes. Spoon syrup over peaches occasionally. Serve warm or cold with whipped cream and a dash of nutmeg.

SPICED FRUIT RESERVE

1 12-oz. pkg. dried apricots
1 12-oz. pkg. dried prunes
1 12-oz. pkg. dried peaches
2 sticks cinnamon
1 fresh orange, sliced
1 fresh lemon, sliced
2 tablespoons whole cloves
2 cups water

Place all ingredients in deep skillet or sauce pan. Add water. Cover and close with lid (if cover has a vent be sure it is closed). Bring to a boil and as soon as fruit starts to boil . . . . cut to simmer and simmer for one hour. This can be prepared in quantity and kept refrigerated to serve anytime.

FRESH PEACH AND PINEAPPLE COMPOTE

⅓ cup sugar
½ cup water
1 tablespoon fresh lemon juice
1 stick whole cinnamon
½ teaspoon whole cloves
¾ teaspoon vanilla extract
2 cups fresh peaches, sliced
2 cups fresh pineapple, diced

Combine sugar, water, lemon juice and cloves in saucepan with the cinnamon stick. Mix well. Boil two minutes. Strain off spices and add vanilla to juice. Fold in the peach slices and pineapple. Chill well . . . . almost to freezing point. Serve in sherbet glasses with a "dollop" of fresh whipped cream (optional).

Fruits and spices go well together. . . . so says the American Spice Trade Association. . . . and to prove it they give us such good ole' suggestions as

BREATH OF SPRING FRESH FRUIT CUP

2 cups fresh strawberries, sliced
1 cup diced fresh pineapple
1 cup fresh grapefruit sections
2 tablespoons fresh lemon juice
¼ cup sugar

Toss all ingredients together **lightly**, and serve in sherbet glasses for dessert. Serves 6.

and the secret ingredient which makes **your** fruit cup different. . . .
¼ teaspoon ground mace

Curried fruit. . . . not fresh from the orchard but right out of the cans on the pantry shelf. . . .

FRUIT CURRY

1 lb. can peach halves
1 lb. can apricot havles
1 lb. can pear halves
1 lb. can pineapple chunks
1 small bottle maraschino cherries
⅓ cup butter
¾ cup firmly packed brown sugar
1 tablespoon curry powder

Drain first five ingredients and place in casserole. Melt butter, brown sugar and curry powder. Blend these and pour over fruit and place in 350°F. oven for about 30 minutes or until real hot and bubbling. Makes one quart and is delicious with any meat dish.

And from New England's countryside comes this recipe for

APPLES IN MAPLE SYRUP

4 good baking apples
½ cup water
1 cup maple syrup
2 tablespoons butter
1 tablespoon cornstarch
½ cup cream
salt (pinch!)

Combine maple syrup and water and boil for 3 minutes. Core and pare apples. Simmer in the boiling syrup until tender. . . . about 20 minutes. When tender remove to a serving bowl and keep warm in oven. Let syrup boil down to about 1 cup. In another pan melt the butter and combine with mixture made with the cornstarch and cream. Cook until thickened and add pinch salt. Pour sauce over apples and serve. (Maybe you'd better double the recipe!)

Georgia may be known as the "peach" state but most folks know that its fast becoming known for its delicious apples too. . . . and anytime is the time to have a delicious

CRISPY APPLE CRUNCH

4 cups of anybody's tart cooking
   apples
1 tablespoon lemon juice
1/2 teaspoon grated lemon peel
1 teaspoon cinnamon
1/2 teaspoon salt
1 cup uncooked oats
1/3 cup sifted all purpose flour
1/2 cup brown sugar
1/2 cup melted butter

Wash, core and slice apples. Place in buttered shallow baking dish. Sprinkle with lemon juice. Combine all other ingredients with butter until crunchy, sprinkle over apples. Bake in 375°F oven for 40 minutes.

Another favorite southern dish. . . . fried apples! If good tart apples are used and fry them just right. . . . MMMMgood. . . .

FRIED APPLES

6-8 medium size tart cooking apples
2/3 cup sugar
1 tablespoon cinnamon
1/4 teaspoon nutmeg
1/3 cup butter
1/8 teaspoon salt

Use a good heavy skillet. Put the butter in skillet over medium heat. Have apples sliced about 1/2 inch thick (remove core before slicing!). Have butter medium hot and place apple slices over bottom skillet. Mix spices and sugar and salt. Sprinkle one half the mixture over apple slices and cook slowly for five minutes. Turn slices and sprinkle remaining sugar mixture over apples. Cook until almost transparent. . . . overcook and slices will break. Serve hot.

BAKED APPLES

6 cooking apples
1/4 cup raisins
1/3 cup orange marmalade
1/2 cup brown sugar
1/2 cup water
1 teaspoon grated lemon peel
1 teaspoon grated orange peel
1/4 cup orange juice
2 tablespoons butter

Core the apples. Combine raisins, and marmalade. Fill center of apples with this mixture. Combine remaining ingredients in saucepan cook over low heat until sugar is dissolved. Simmer five minutes. Pour this syrup over apples which have been placed in a baking dish. Bake at 350°F for 45 minutes to an hour. Baste often. When tender. . . baste. . . and run under broiler to glaze. Serve warm with whipped cream.

Cranberries....good fruit....city cookin or "Country Cookin" for instance....make your own CRANBERRY SAUCE....

4 cups fresh cranberries
2 cups sugar
1-2 cups water

Combine all ingredients in saucepan. Heat to a boiling point, stirring until sugar dissolves. Then boil rapidly until berries pop open (usually takes about a minute). Makes one quart cranberry sauce. Pour into hot sterilized jars....seal with ¼ inch parafin wax and tight lid or store in tightly covered container in refrigerator for several weeks.

Another delicious cranberry recipe....great with meats of all kinds....especially good for your holiday buffet....

BRANDIED CRANBERRIES

1 pkg. (usually 1 lb. or 4 cups)
    fresh cranberries
2 cups sugar
⅓ cup apricot brandy

Wash and remove stems from cranberries. Place on baking sheet (jelly roll pan....one with sides!) Pour sugar over and place in oven....medium heat 325°F. **Cover with aluminum foil** before placing in oven! Cook until sugar melts and cranberries begin to pop. Cranberries should be tender but not mushy. Pour into large bowl and pour brandy over. Stir with "fold over" strokes until berries are saturated with brandy. Cover and set aside until cool. Place in refrigerator....makes good gifts for neighbors....put in condiment jars with lids and your own "from the kitchen of...." sticker!

The
Soup Kettle

SOUP KETTLE

Remember that ole story from your childhood days that spoke of "hard times" and nothing from which to make a kettle of soup? But an enterprising villager. . . one never to give up. . . came up with the great idea of developing a very original soup. The base for the soup? A rock! A smooth stone, which he washed and washed. . . placed it in a kettle of water, added a little salt and then. . . asked the villagers, one by one, to add to it. One gave a carrot, another potatoes, another cabbage and so on. And the end result? A kettle full of delicious soup. . . enough to feed everybody! Like that story? It has several variations, incidentally! Just like soups. . . everybody has his favorite. We hope you'll find some of ours to be some of yours!

Note: One of the best things about soup. . . you can always make a big kettle full. . . eat what you want. . . share with neighbors (take along a loaf of your favorite homemade bread with it!), and then freeze the remainder in serving size containers. . . and you're ready for the next cold day which comes along. . . with something zesty to eat! From the Soup Kettle!

Just a good ole'bean soup. . . . great for those cold winter days. . . . served with hot homemeade bread and a pat of fresh churned butter!

BEAN SOUP

½ pound beans (I prefer small navy beans)
1 tablespoon vinegar
1 small white onion
3 fresh green onions
½ pound bacon (unsliced)
1 teaspoon sugar
6 cups water
1 stalk celery (finely chopped)
2 sprigs parsley (finely chopped)
1 bay leaf
salt and fresh ground black pepper to taste

Wash beans and soak overnight. Drain off water. Place the bacon piece in a heavy kettle. Cook until fat covers bottom of kettle. Add the onion (white and fresh green onions) (be sure to use a portion of the green tops!). Saute until soft. Add the vinegar, sugar, water, celery and parsley. Bring to a boil and put the beans in mixture. Add the bay leaf and simmer for about 1-1½ hours. Before serving remove the bacon and the bay leaf. Serve in ceramic or earthenware bowls of any type.

Note: A few crushed red peppers may be added toward end of cooking. . . . for extra zest! If soup becomes too thick, add another cup of water while cooking.

The Minnesota Historical Society is responsible for this. . . .

OLD FASHIONED TURKEY SOUP

3 quarts turkey (or chicken) stock
¼ cup finely diced, cooked turkey (or more, if you desire)
3 large onions
3 stalks celery
2 medium sized carrots
½ pound butter
1½ cups flour
1 pint light cream
¼ cup cooked rice
salt and pepper to taste

Chop onions, celery and carrots very fine. Cook with a little water for 20 minutes or until tender. Melt butter and blend in flour thoroughly. Heat stock and cream and add very gradually to butter and flour mixture, stirring until lumps disappear. Add vegetables, water, salt and pepper. Stir and cook over low heat for 10 minutes. Add turkey and rice. makes about 4 quarts of soup.

Note: To make your turkey or chicken stock, add 3 quarts of water and 1 tablespoon salt to cooked carcass or raw necks and wings. Simmer for several hours and strain.

From our Italian friends comes a most delicious recipe for a popular family soup. . . . serve it **hot** with grated Parmesan cheese sprinkled generously on each serving.

MINESTRONE SOUP

1 pound fresh peas
1 cup celery, diced
2 carrots, diced
1 large onion, sliced
1 cup canned tomatoes
¾ pound fine spaghetti, vermicelli
3 quarts water
3 potatoes, diced
½ teaspoon salt
⅛ teaspoon pepper
oil for cooking vegetables

Clean vegetables. Saute onions and potatoes in hot oil about 10 minutes or until medium brown. Add tomatoes, salt and pepper; cover; cook slowly about 15 minutes.
In a separate pot, bring to a boil 3 quarts of water. Add celery, peas, and carrots; cover and cook 15 minutes or until vegetables are tender. Add all other ingredients and the spaghetti, broken into 1" pieces. Cover and cook 20 minutes. Serves 6-8.

TOMATO CORN CHOWDER

4 cups canned tomatoes, undrained
4 cups canned corn, cream-style
¼ teaspoon baking soda
3 slices fat salt pork, diced
    (slices about ¼" thick)
1 medium onion, sliced
3 medium potatoes, peeled
    and diced
1 teaspoon salt
6 cups hot milk
⅛ teaspoon pepper

Fry salt pork in heavy kettle until brown. Add onion and continue cooking for 5 minutes. Boil potatoes until tender in just enough water to cover, adding the teaspoon of salt. Do not drain, but add salt pork and onion with the fat from the frying pan. Add corn and tomatoes. Heat until very hot and add soda. When frothing subsides, add hot milk and season with pepper and a little more salt if desired. Serves 6.

If you like a good hearty oyster soup.... try this recipe for

OYSTER BISQUE

1 dozen large raw oysters	Drain oysters. Reserve 1 cup liq-
1 cup oyster liquor	uor. Dice oysters into saucepan
3 cups milk	and add liquer. Bring to a boil,
2 cup heavy cream	slowly. When boiling point is
1 slice of onion	reached, remove from heat and
2 stalks celery	pour oysters into a bowl and set
1 sprig parsley	aside. In same saucepan, scald the
1 bay leaf	milk and cream with onion,
⅓ cup butter, melted	celery, parsley and bay leaf.
⅓ cup flour	Strain. Blend butter with flour, salt
1¾ teaspoons salt	and Tabasco. Slowly stir in scaled
½ teaspoon Tabasco	milk. Stir over low heat until it is
chopped chives	thickened. Add oysters and cook-
	ing liquid. Heat to a serving
	temperature. Garnish with chop-
	ped chives.

SOME QUICK SOUPS - TANTALIZING AND TASTY!

Take a can of cream of mushroom soup with onions, add a can of chicken broth and ¼ cup Sherry.... Heat and eat!

A can of cream of chicken soup blended with a can of split pea soup, add ¼ cup finely chopped green onion, the barest suggestion of nutmeg.... Heat until well blended and serve with toasted croutons!

A can of chicken broth, blended with ½ cup chopped artichoke hearts, ½ cup cream and a dash of chervil.... Unusual.... Serve hot!

A can of tomato soup, diluted with cream, dash of oregano.... Serve with toasted crackers.... Hot!

Jackie Jeffries shared this recipe with us for....

POTATO SOUP

Boil one large hen in 2 quarts water with 1 bay leaf, 1 medium onion (chop-ped), salt and pepper to taste. When chicken is tender, remove from broth and cool. Add 8 medium Irish potatoes to broth (cut in cubes before hand). Cook until tender. In separate pan melt ½ pound butter and make a sauce with a little flour, salt and pepper. Add to broth (a little at a time so will not be lumpy), stir until thickened. Remove chicken from bone. Cube pieces and add to soup. Serve piping hot. Add another dash of coarsely ground black pepper on each serving. MMMmmmmmmmmm!

Another good soup for a blustery winter day. . . .

ONION SOUP

1 tablespoon butter
1 teaspoon bacon drippings
4 cups chopped onions
2 10½ oz. cans beef consomme
10½ oz. water
    (consomme can filled)
salt and pepper to taste
¼ cup Brandy

Melt butter in a heavy pot. Add bacon drippings and onions and brown. Add beef consomme and water. Bring to a boil. Reduce heat and simmer for an hour. Add ¼ cup Brandy (alcohol is removed when heated but leaves a delightful taste!). Simmer for another 15 minutes.
When ready to serve. . . . top each individual ovenproof bowl with a slice of toasted bread, about 1 inch thick. On top of the bread sprinkle grated Gruyere and Parmesan Cheese. . . . sprinkle generously! Place bowls under broiler until cheese is brown and bubbly. Serve immediately.

Great with a Gardens Salad and maybe a thick slice of your favorite homemade bread.

Some like it hot. . . . some like it cold, you'll like this recipe either way. From the land of Tabasco, Avery Island. . . .

EASY VICHYSSOISE

1 can condensed cream of potato
    soup
2 cups milk (maybe use 1 cup
    cream and 1 cup milk)
½ teaspoon salt
¼ teaspoon Tabasco
1 small cucumber pared and diced
    (should have about 1½ cups)
2 tablespoons chopped parsley or
    chives

Combine soup, milk, salt and Tabasco in saucepan. Bring to a boil, stirring occasionally. Remove from heat, stir in diced cucumber. Serve hot or chilled. Garnish with finely chopped chives or parsley on top of soup. Serves 4.

Irene DuBose, Stewart County Extension Agent says the following is one of the "heartiest, easy to make soups she's every served her family". She's a mighty good cook, so we suggest next time you want something good to eat. . . try her Oxtail or Stewmeat Soup!

OXTAIL or STEWMEAT SOUP

1½ lbs. oxtails or stewmeat
2 large onions, chopped
2 teaspoons salt (or salt to taste)
2 ribs celery, chopped or 2
teas   poons celery flakes
2 quarts water
pepper to taste (½ teaspoon)
2 teaspoon seasoning salt
2 beef bouillon cubes
1 pint vegetable soup mixture or 1
    no. 2 can mixed vegetables
1 can cream of tomato soup or
    tomato juice

Combine meat, onion, salt, celery, pepper and water, bring to a boil and simmer until meat is tender enough to remove from bones (2 hours or more). Add more water if needed. Remove meat and take out bones, cut meat into small pieces, return to broth, add seasoning salt, bouillon cubes and vegetables. Cook until vegetables are tender. Add tomato soup or tomato juice, bring to a boil. Stir and serve hot with crackers or cornbread. I serve a cheese sandwich and a beverage with this for a complete meal.

Somewhere we found this recipe for a very satisfying soup. . and a very generous bowl only has 100 calories in it. And yet it is very nutritious.

LOW CALORIE VEGETABLE SOUP

2 pound beef soup bone
4 stalks celery, diced
3 carrots, diced
1 medium onion, chopped
1 cup turnips, diced
    (or rutabagas)
2 cups raw cabbage, cut up,
    rather fine (not as much as
    for slaw)
½ cup green peas
½ cup tomatoes, chopped
    (canned or fresh)
1 tablespoon barley, raw
1 teaspoon salt
4 whole kernels black peppers
    (peppercorns)
4 kernels whole allspice
water, to make desired consistency

Cook soup bone until you can remove all meat from bone. Add all other ingredients to the soup stock and place in a heavy kettle. Bring to a boil and cook slowly until vegetables are done. You may want to add a dash of crushed red peppers to add a little more zest.

SPARE RIB SOUP

2½ pounds spare ribs, cut in
    serving pieces
1 pound dried Lima beans
1 #2 can tomatoes
2 medium potatoes, cut fine
2 carrots, diced
1 medium onion, finely chopped
2 stalks celery, chopped
salt and pepper

Pre-boil spare ribs in lightly salted water until slightly tender. (Skim any foam from water). Then add above ingredients and bring to a boil, simmer about 2 hours or until beans are soft. Add any additional salt and pepper needed. Serves 6.

Simply great! Serve with hot buttered bread, a salad and dessert!

Mrs. Mildred Davis, organist for Callaway Gardens in the beautiful Ida Cason Callaway Chapel, is also a fantastic gourmet cook. How she finds time for it, I don't know...since she and her husband, Alvin, also own and run the "Davis Inn" at Pine Mountain. But somehow she works it all in and the result is pure enjoyment...in the Chapel...the Inn...or the kitchen...we prevailed upon her to share with us a recipe highly recommended by Pat Collins, from the Horticulture Department at the Gardens. She calls it. . . .

WILD WESTERN CHILI SOUP

1 tablespoon oil
1½ pounds ground beef
1 teaspoon salt
1 cup chopped onion
½ teaspoon garlic powder
2 cans beef broth
2 cans tomato soup
2 cans kidney beans (1 lb. cans)
    (do not drain beans)
2 tablespoons chili powder
2 tablespoons vinegar (Apple
    Cider Vinegar)
2 cups cooked elbow macaroni
    (about ¾ cups uncooked is
    right)

In deep skillet put oil, ground beef, salt, onion and garlic powder. Brown and cover with tight lid. Cook until meat is almost done. Add all other ingredients and simmer for 30 minutes on very low heat. Serve hot with slaw and cornbread. Mighty good!

The Herb Garden and Salad Greens

THE HERB GARDEN AND SALAD GREENS

One of the most delightful spots in "Mr. Cason's Garden"....is the Herb Garden....sage, thyme, marjoram, sweet basil, parsley and rosemary...."For remembrance"....and many others. Fresh herbs are such a delight to use in so many recipes because they give instant action. A pleasure to grow and to dry....incidentally, herbs need to be stored in air-tight containers when dried. Ground herbs are among the more fragile products on the spice shelf.

As for those salad greens grown in the garden....they're like a bit of sunshine served on a moment's notice, also....remember one of the secrets of a good salad (in addition to nice, crisp, fresh greens) is a well seasoned salad bowl. Never, never soak your salad bowl. Rinse with warm water **only**. Some people won't even touch with water....they just wipe it dry with paper towels..knowing that, in time, the garlic and the onion will season the bowl and help add a delightful flavor to the salad!

From the Herb Gardens. . . . "Rosemary for Remembrance". . . . and anyone who tastes these onions with this special glaze will never forget the taste!

ROSEMARY-GLAZED ONIONS

3 lbs. small white onions, peeled
1/3 cup sugar
2 teaspoons lemon juice
1/2 teaspoon dried rosemary leaves
salt to taste
1/4 cup butter

Cook onions in about an inch of boiling water with 2 teaspoons salt. Bring onions to boiling point. Reduce the heat and simmer, covered for about 20 minutes. Watch carefully and do not over-cook, but have semi-tender. Drain. Keep hot while you make a glaze. In a large skillet, combine the butter, sugar, lemon juice and rosemary. Stir with wooden spoon until sugar dissolves and mixture reaches boiling point. Add onions. Cook uncovered for about 10 minutes. Turn onions several times until they are well glazed.

This will become one of your favorite recipes. . . . For Sunday supper or special company. Serves about 12.

Try marjoram as an ideal herb for your salad. . . . One of Shakespeare's characters spoke of marjoram in this way: "We may pick a thousands salads ere we light on such another herb"! Try this Herbed Crab Meat Salad.

HERBED CRAB SALAD

8 oz. can flaked crab meat (1 cup cooked fresh or canned)
2 medium fresh tomatoes, diced
3/4 cup chopped celery
1/8 teaspoon instant garlic powder
1/2 teaspoon ground marjoram
1/8 teaspoon black pepper
1 1/4 teaspoon salt
2 teaspoons sugar
1 tablespoon salad oil
1 tablespoon vinegar
2 tablespoons mayonnaise

Mix crab meat, tomatoes and celery. Place in large bowl. Blend all other ingredients. Toss with crab meat mixture and serve on crisp lettuce leaf. Serves 5-6.

From the world's great Bernard L. Lewis Spices. . . . come these quick tips for using herbs:

CUMIN BUTTER

Blend ¼ teaspoon ground Cumin with ¼ cup melted butter. Great served over hot cooked corn-on-the-cob.

SWEET BASIL BEANS

Cook beans in lightly salted water. When tender add 2 tablespoons butter per pound beans and add ½ teaspoon sweet basil per pound beans. Delightful flavor!

CARROTS OR WINTER SQUASH WITH ALLSPICE

Ground Allspice is a delightful spice with carrots or winter squash, use about ⅛ teaspoon per 2 cups vegetables. Add to last five minutes of cooking time.

HERB BUTTER

⅓ pound butter
1 tablespoon parsley, finely chopped
1 tablespoon chopped chives or
    scallions
1 tablespoon sweet basil (fresh)
    less if dried
½ teaspoon lemon juice
⅛ teaspoon Tabasco

Soften butter. Mix with the herbs and seasonings. Great with French Bread. Slice bread and spread with herb butter. Wrap in foil and heat. Great also with green vegetables. . . . 'specially green beans!

CABBAGE WITH CARAWAY SEED

1 medium head cabbage
½ teaspoon salt
½ teaspoon sugar
¼ cup onion flakes
1½ teaspoon salt
⅛ tablespoon black pepper
1 tablespoon butter
½ teaspoon caraway seed
1 tablespoon lemon juice

Shred cabbage and place in saucepan with about 1 inch boiling water, ½ teaspoon salt, sugar and onion flakes. Boil uncovered five minutes. Cover and boil until cabbage is tender (about 3 minutes). Drain. Add 1½ teaspoon salt, black pepper, butter, caraway seed and lemon juice. Serve piping hot.

Who doesn't love the taste of "Wilted Lettuce".... a recipe as old as the hills and takes no time to prepare.... you just take

2 cups garden lettuce (tear it into bite size)
6 garden fresh green onions (cut into small pieces with stems included!)
5 strips bacon
6 tablespoons vinegar
6 tablespoons water
salt and pepper to taste
1 tablespoon sugar
2 hard cooked eggs, sliced

Mix the eggs with the lettuce. Fry bacon until very crisp. Remove from pan, drain and crumble. Combine the vinegar, water, salt and pepper and sugar with the bacon drippings. Heat to boiling and then add the crumbled bacon and chopped onion. Mix well and pour over lettuce. Toss lightly and serve quickly.

SPINACH SALAD

1 pound fresh, tender, crisp spinach
Dressing:
¾ cup French Dressing
8 slices bacon
3 hard cooked eggs
1 clove garlic

Tear spinach into pieces. Place in large salad bowl.
Peel and cut in quarters 1 clove garlic. Place it in the French Dressing. Cook the bacon until crisp. Drain on paper towel. Crumble and add to the crisp spinach. Add the eggs which have been finely chopped. Remove the garlic pieces from the dressing and toss greens with dressing. Serve immediately. Makes generous servings for six.

CUCUMBER SALAD

2 medium unpeeled cucumbers
1½ teaspoons salt
2 tablespoons cider vinegar
⅛ teaspoon crushed red pepper
⅓ cup chopped green onions
¾ cup sour cream

Cut cucumbers in ⅛ inch slices. Add salt and vinegar. Mix well. Let stand 2 hours. Drain. Add crushed red pepper, onions and toss lightly with sour cream. Serve at once. Serves 5.

Tops on the salad list. . . . CAESAR'S SALAD! From our friends at Sunkist. This is a real luncheon treat! Serve generously!

4 quarts crisp, chilled lettuce
1 teaspoon salt
1 tablespoon Worcestershire sauce
fresh ground black pepper
1 egg
4 tablespoons fresh lemon juice
2 tablespoons wine vinegar
1 cup croutons
½ cup & 2 tablespoons garlic
    flavored salad oil
8 tablespoons grated Parmesan
    Cheese

Tear lettuce into medium sized pieces. Place in large chilled bowl. Sprinkle with salt and Worcestershire sauce. Sprinkle generously with fresh ground black pepper. Add egg and pour lemon juice and vinegar on top of it. Add croutons and toss lightly. Pour garlic flavored salad oil onto it and toss lightly. Sprinkle with Parmesan cheese. Serve immediately.

Take two old "stand bys", like grapefruit and broccoli. . . . ever tried serving them in a salad? Our Sunkist Home Economist says "Try it, you'll like it".

BROCCOLI AND GRAPEFRUIT SALAD

1 grapefruit
2 pounds fresh broccoli
1 cup bottled Italian Dressing
¼ cup fresh squeezed lemon juice
¼ cup sliced pitted black olives
1 tablespoon pimento strips

Peel and section grapefruit, reserve juice. Drain and refrigerate sections. Clean and trim broccoli. Cook until **just** tender, about 10 and not more than 15 minutes. Drain carefully and place in shallow dish. Combine dressing and lemon juice, pour over hot broccoli. Cover and chill until very cold (at least two hours). Chill remaining ingredients. When ready to serve, arrange broccoli spears on platter or individual serving dishes. Add grapefruit sections. Garnish with black olives and pimento strips. Serves 6.

Note: reserved grapefruit juice may be used instead of lemon juice.

The Georgia Egg Commission Home Economists have some great recipes, we especially like this one for:

GARDEN EGG SALAD

8 hard cooked eggs
½ cup mayonnaise
⅓ cup sweet pickle relish
¼ teaspoon celery seed
½ teaspoon instant minced onion
    you may use ⅓ cup finely
    chopped green onion
1 pkg., 10 oz., frozen green peas
¼ cup chopped celery
lettuce leaves

Stir together mayonnaise, relish, celery seed and finely chopped or instant onion. Toss with eggs, peas and celery. Cover and chill until flavors are well blended. Serve on lettuce leaves. Makes 8 servings. Serve with toasted crackers.

You may garnish top of individual salads with a dash of paprika.

MIXED GREEN SALAD

2 cups watercress
1 cup leaf lettuce
2 tomatoes, firm
Roquefort Dressing:
1¼ oz. soft Roquefort Cheese
¼ cup salad oil
2 tablespoons lemon juice
3 tablespoons Sherry wine
½ tablespoon Worcestershire sauce
salt and pepper to taste

Shred lettuce into pieces and cut tomatoes into wedges. Toss lightly together.

Blend cheese and oil until smooth. Add other ingredients and mix well. Absolutely great with greens! Serve on Mixed Green Salad.

A good salad has eye appeal as well as taste appeal and a shrimp salad needs the crisp fresh look (and taste) of lettuce . . . . any kind!

SHRIMP SALAD

1 pound fresh cooked shrimp
2 cups sliced celery
1/4 teaspoon salt
2 teaspoons sugar
1/2 teaspoon dry mustard
1/8 teaspoon paprika
2 teaspoon horseradish
1/8 teaspoon Tabasco *
2 tablespoons vinegar
1/3 cup cooking oil

Prepare shrimp. Mix with celery. Mix salt, sugar, dry mustard and paprika. Add horseradish, cooking oil and vinegar. Blend well. Pour over shrimp and chill for two hours. Add celery. Serve on a beautiful crisp lettuce leaf. Garnish with a bit of parsley.

*Tabasco is optional, may be zesty enough with just the horseradish, but, if you like it a little "hotter" . . . . add the Tabasco . . . .

Here's a plain, simple molded gelatin salad, good any time, 'specially good in the summer months . . . . cool, delicious, nutritious and refreshing!

MOLDED VEGETABLE SALAD

1 package lemon gelatin (Jello)
1½ cups drained cooked mixed vegetables
1/3 cup salad dressing
1/2 cup chopped celery
1½ teaspoons grated onion
1 cup hot water
2/3 cup cold water

Pour salad dressing over vegetables and let stand 2 hours to marinate. Dissolve gelatin in hot water. Add cold water and chill until slightly thickened. Then fold in marinated vegetables, onion and celery. Pour into ring mold and chill until firm. Unmold and garnish with salad greens.

You may want to serve a little salad dressing mixed with a small amount of fresh lemon juice and a dash of paprika.

The Pickle Crock

THE PICKLE CROCK

Sweet pickles, dill pickles, sour pickles, pickled peppers. . . . all memories of the old fashioned "Pickle Crock". Ever sneak that "rock off the crock" (that rock which held the plate in place on top of the crock) and sneak out a big, plump, juicy pickle? (Maybe even tasting of a little brine!) Just nothing like it. Pickle making begins with the first tiny cucumbers to come off the vines. . . . and if you "tend" them right, those vines just keep on producing throughout the summer. So, anytime is Pickle Time. And if you have just enough room in the yard for a couple of vines. . . . you'll have plenty of cucumbers, or you may do as some other folks do and plant a couple of vines in a keg. Looks pretty and does pretty well, too. . . . keeping fresh cucumbers on the table. . . . or pickles in the Pickle Crock. . . .

Everybody loved Mama's green tomato-onion relish. . . . we share it with you. . . .

TOMATO-ONION RELISH

20 green tomatoes
4 bell peppers
4-5 red hot peppers
8 onions
6 apples
3 cups vinegar
3 cups sugar
1 teaspoon cloves
1 teaspoon mustard seed
1 teaspoon allspice

Chop tomatoes, peppers, onions and apples into small pieces (may use chop setting on your blender or use your food processor). Combine with all remaining ingredients and cook over low heat for about two hours. Put into sterilized jars and seal.

Ripe tomatoes may be substituted for green ones, if desired.

Helen Joerg's delightfully crisp sweet pickles. . . . something you'll want to keep on hand all year. . . . this is a **different** recipe!

QUICK AND EASY PICKLES

1 gallon sour or dill pickles
5 pounds sugar
1 box pickling spices

Remove pickles from juice and drain well. Slice into ¼ inch slices. Pour slices into crock or large pottery bowl (may also use stainless steel bowl, but not aluminum). Pour the sugar and the spices over and toss until well covered. Cover the container tightly with aluminum foil. Toss frequently for **three** days (you'll want to set the container in a cool place). After three days. . . . lift the pickles from the juice and strain juice. . . . put the pickle slices back in the juice and repeat three times. . . . straining the juice each time in order to remove most of the spices. Then lift slices into jars and cover with the clean juice. Store in the refrigerator. We haven't tried sealing these for the pantry shelf but you might try a few. . . . placing the pickles in a sterilized jar and sealing tightly. . . . watch for any fermentation.

No country garden would be complete without rows of okra . . . . one of our favorite ways of having this delicious vegetable throughout the year is

PICKLED OKRA

Select small, tender pods of okra (from the garden or farmers market). We'll give you the recipe for 1 quart . . . . you may want to triple it and pack in pints . . . . anyway for a quart jar you'll need:

1 tablespoon dried dill seed
1 pod garlic, chopped
2 small pods red hot pepper
⅛ teaspoon alum
1 cup white vinegar
2 cups water
¼ cup salt
1 teaspoon mustard seed

Pack okra in jar (or jars). Mix your dill seed, chopped garlic, alum, mustard seed and whole peppers in with okra. Mix vinegar, water and salt and bring to a boil. Pour over okra until jar is filled over top of okra. Seal tightly and set aside for at least two weeks for best flavor.

GREEN TOMATO PICKLES

1 gallon green tomatoes, chopped
1 cup salt
2 medium onions
½ medium head cabbage
4 large green peppers
2 large sweet red peppers
3 cups vinegar
2 cups high-grade molasses
2 teaspoons celery seed
2 teaspoons mustard seed
1 teaspoon whole cloves in a bag

Mix tomatoes with salt and let stand overnight. Drain. Put other vegetables through a food chopper, using a coarse blade. Place tomatoes and chopped vegetables in a large kettle. Add vinegar and remaining ingredients. Cook mixture until tender and quite thick. About 35 minutes. Remove cloves. Pour into sterilized jars and seal.

Comes late summer and the pears ripen . . . . and one of the most sought after recipes when the pears are plentiful is one for

PEAR RELISH

12 large pears
12 bell peppers (some red, some green)
2 cups sugar
1 teaspoon salt
1 quart vinegar
3 large onions
several green and red hot peppers, if desired, (and I do desire!)

Run the pears, peppers and onions through meat chopper (or, if you have a modern food processor . . . . its great for this!). Use medium blade if you are using the meat chopper. Cook all ingredients together until tender. Pour into hot sterilized jars and seal while hot. Its an old recipe but a great one . . . . you'll love this relish with vegetables or meats.

WATERMELON PICKLES

7 lbs. watermelon (cut into strips about ¼ inch square)
2 cups household lime
1 4-oz. box alum
5 lbs. sugar
5 pints cider vinegar
1 teaspoon ground allspice
1 teaspoon mustard seed
1 box stick cinnamon
1 box mixed pickling spices
1 teaspoon whole cloves

Prepare watermelon rind by peeling and cutting as above. Mix 2 cups lime in 2 gallons water (mix well). Pour over the watermelon, cover and let stand for 24 hours. Drain well, wash several times in clear water. Mix 4 ounce box alum in 2 gallons water (mix well), pour over watermelon, cover and let stand for 24 hours. Drain and wash several times in clear water. Soak pieces 4 hours in clear water, changing the water every hour. Drain well! Tie mixed pickling spices in thin cloth (unless your prefer the various spices mixed through the pickles) place in saucepan with sugar, vinegar, allspice, cloves and mustard seed. Bring to a boil and pour over watermelon rind. Let stand overnight. Drain and bring liquid to a boil and drop rind in slowly in order not to stop the boiling. Boil for 20-30 minutes. Place in hot jars. Add a small amount of stick cinnamon to each jar. Seal tightly.

MUSTARD PICKLES

1 quart cucumber slices
1 quart small onions
1 quart small pickles
1 quart string beans
1 quart green tomatoes
6 green peppers
1 head cauliflower, in flowerets, or chopped

Small vegetables should be selected, as they are more attractive if they remain whole. Put all in strong salt water for 24 hours. Drain, heat the liquid, scald the vegetables with it, and drain again. Make a dressing with the following:

DRESSING

6 tablespoons mustard
1 tablespoon tumeric
1 cup sugar
1 cup flour
2 quarts vinegar

Boil unti thick and then add the above pickles. Let boil from 3-5 minutes, but do not allow the pickles to get soft. Put pickles in hot sterilized jars and pour dressing over. Seal tightly.

Everybody has a favorite bread and butter pickle . . . . we've tried may, but finally decided that this one from Scottsboro, Alabama might be the one to include in "Country Cookin". . . .

BREAD AND BUTTER PICKLES

7 pounds cucumbers-sliced (please use the small cucumbers)
2 gallons water
2 cups lime
4½ pounds sugar
½ gallon vinegar
1 teaspoon cloves
2 tablespoons pickling spices
⅓ cup plain salt
1 teaspoon celery seed

Soak the sliced cucumbers in lime and water for 24 hours. Stir occasionally. Wash in cold water and let stand for 3 hours. Mix sugar, spices, vinegar and salt and pour over drained sliced cucumbers and let stand overnight. Place mixture in kettle and simmer for 35 minutes. Place in jars and seal. Chill well before serving.

ONION SAUCE

2 gallon skinned, chopped, ripe tomatoes
½ gallon chopped onions
2 tablespoons salt
1 cup sugar
6 green hot peppers, finely chopped
2 pints vinegar (more if needed)

Mix all ingredients. Let come to a rolling boil and turn down to simmer. Simmer for 45 minutes. Pour into hot sterilized jars and seal.

QUICK CORN RELISH

4 cups whole kernel corn, canned
1 cup sweet pickle relish
½ cup red pepper relish
¼ teaspoon red crushed pepper
salt and black pepper to taste

Drain all the ingredients well and mix together. Add the crushed red pepper, salt and black pepper. Mix well and chill thoroughly before serving.

Those little red berries from New England States are the base ingredient in some mighty delicious recipes. We like this one for

CRANBERRY RELISH

1 can (1 lb.) jellied cranberry sauce
½ cup applesauce
¼ cup raisins
½ teaspoon cinnamon

Mix all the ingredients well. Chill and serve as an accompaniment to pork, chicken or beef.

Change the recipe a little and have a delicious accompaniment for fish:

1 can whole berry cranberry sauce
¼ cup drained sweet pickle relish
1 tablespoon prepared horseradish

Blend all ingredients well and chill before serving with any fish dish.

The Jelly Jar

THE JELLY JAR

Back in the "good ole' days"...jellies and jams were only made "in season"...when fruits were ripe. The spring and summer days were just filled with pickin' and washin' berries and fruits to make up into delicious concoctions for the winter days ahead. Blackberries..Dewberries..Cherries..Plums (wild ones are the best for jelly!)..Apples..Peaches and Pears! Watermelon and Rhubarb came in for their share of preserves, too. Fact is...jellies and jams were made with somewhat "loving, tender care"...because fruits had to be picked and made up right away or else they would spoil with the warm weather. For the most part sugar was the thickening agent...no Sure-Jell and pectin available in those days! But now...times have changed. Science has done some mighty good things for the world of food, and one result is in the area of jams and jellies. We can make fresh jars all year long. Just freeze the juice when the fruit is ripe, get a box or bottle of pectin...go by directions.. and "presto" in a minute...beautiful food for the breakfast table or for gifts.. your own special "Jelly Jars"!

Jellies, jams, marmalades, conserves, preserves. . . . what is the difference?

Jelly: is a clear, sweet spread made from fruit juice, pectin and sugar.
Jam: is a thick, sweet spread with pieces of crushed or chopped fruit.
Marmalade: looks like jam, but has chopped fruit and citrus rind in it.
Conserve: is a combination of fruits plus nuts and raisins.
Preserves: small whole fruits, or uniform pieces, in clear syrup.

When General Foods came out with Sure-Jell. . . . it was the greatest thing which could ever have happened to jelly and jam making! No more cooking and cooking over a hot stove and then. . . . sometimes have jelly which wouldn't "jell"! Think how easy it is now to always have a cupboard full of such delicious goodies as

FREEZER FRUIT CUP JAM

¾ cup prepared strawberries (about 1 pint)
¾ cup prepared pineapple (¼ ripe fresh pineapple or ¾ cup crushed, drained, canned pineapple
½ cup chopped oranges (remove peel, membrane and seeds)
½ cup pears (peel, core and grind about ½ lb. fully ripe pears)
4½ cups sugar (2 lbs.)
¾ cup water or juice from pineapple (if canned used)
1 box Sure-Jell

Thoroughly crush strawberries and mix with prepared pineapple, oranges and pears. Mix sugar into the fruits and set aside. Mix Sure-Jell with water in a small pan. Bring to a boil and boil for one minute, stirring constantly. Stir into fruits and continue stirring for three minutes. Ladle quickly into jars. Cover at once with tight lids. Let stand for 24 hours or until "set". Store in freezer or if to be used within 2 or 3 weeks, store in refrigerator. Makes 6 medium size jars. And when you open it up. . . . it's delightfully fresh tasting! (Another good gift from "your kitchen").

Rhubarb! A special treat from an old fashioned garden (and sometimes to be found in your favorite grocery!) Its great in pies and a very special delicacy in

RHUBARB JAM

2½ pounds fresh rhubarb
1 cup water
few drops red food coloring
6½ cups sugar (2 lbs., 14 oz.)
1 box Sure-Jell

Chop fresh rhubarb into small pieces (unpeeled!). Color with few drops of red food coloring if not naturally red. Add the cup of water and bring to a boil. Simmer uncovered until rhubarb is soft (takes about one minute). Measure 4½ cups of it into **large** saucepan. Add Sure-Jell to rhubarb. Mix well. Bring to a hard boil, stirring constantly. When boiling hard, quickly add sugar and bring to a full rolling boil and boil hard for **one minute** . . . . stir constantly. Remove from heat and skim off any foam. Stir and skin for about five minutes to keep fruit from floating. Ladle quickly into 8 medium glasses. Cover with about ⅛ inch hot paraffin and seal.

CRANBERRY-MINT JELLY

4½ cups sugar
2 pints Cranberry Juice Cocktail
1 box powdered pectin (Sure-Jell)
1⅛ teaspoons peppermint extract
paraffin

Place Cranberry Juice Cocktail in large saucepan. Add one box pectin. Place over high heat and bring to a rolling boil. Quickly stir in sugar, all at once. Bring to full rolling boil again. Boil hard for **one minute**, stirring constantly. Remove from heat, add peppermint extract. Skim. Pour quickly into 8 sterilized glasses. Pour melted paraffin over at once (¼ inch) and seal tightly.

One of the nicest places to visit at Callaway Gardens is Mr. Cason's Vegetable Garden....one that almost knows "no season"....something is always growing there....and a favorite spot....is the Herb Garden....rows and rows and bunches and bunches....if you have access to such....gather some herbs and make

HERB JELLY

4 tablespoons dried herbs, crushed
   (could be sage, thyme,
   tarragon, marjoram or a
   combination of all)
2½ cups boiling water
¼ cup vinegar
4½ cups sugar (2 lbs.)
½ bottle Certo fruit pectin
green food coloring

Pour boiling water over herbs. Let stand about 20 minutes. Strain and measure 2 cups into large pan. Add vinegar and sugar to herb water. Mix well. Bring to a boil over high heat. Stir constantly adding food coloring to desired shade. When at a high boil, add Certo fruit pectin at once. Bring to a full rolling boil and boil hard for **one minute,** stirring constantly. Remove from heat, skim off foam and pour into glasses. Cover with ⅛ inch hot paraffin and seal. Makes 6 medium glasses. Sooo good with meats.!

CALIFORNIA ORANGE MARMALADE

3 medium oranges, unpeeled,
   thinly sliced into half cart-
   wheels (3 cups)
1 medium lemon, unpeeled,
   thinly sliced into half cart-
   wheels (¾ cup)
3 quarts cold water
sugar

Combine orange and lemon slices and water in large glass bowl; cover and let stand 12 hours, or overnight. Place in deep, heavy saucepan and bring to a boil; boil hard for 30 minutes until reduced to about 8 cups. Let stand 6-8 hours. Measure fruit and liquid; add an equal amount of sugar. Bring to a boil, stirring until sugar dissolves. Boil rapidly until mixture sheets from a spoon when tested, approximately 30 minutes. Gently stir occasionally to avoid sticking. Remove from heat; stir and skim for 5 minutes. Pour into hot sterilized jars and seal with paraffin.

Damson plums! A garden would not have been complete without at least a couple of plum trees. . . . so good to eat. . . . makes such delicious preserves, conserves, jams and pies! We selected this one for you to try from our favorite "Country Cookin" recipes. . . . tested in the General Foods Kitchens. . . .

DAMSON PLUM CONSERVE

2 pounds Damson Plums
    (fully ripe)
1 orange
2 cups water
½ cup seedless raisins
7 cups sugar (3 lbs.)
1 box Sure-Jell fruit pectin
½ cup walnuts (coarsly chopped)

Chop the orange very, very fine, add water and simmer (covered) for about 20 minutes. Pit, but do not peel, and halve the fully ripe plums. Chop fine. Combine fruits and measure 4½ cups into a very large saucepan. Add raisins. Mix Sure-Jell into fruit. Bring to a hard boil over high heat. Stir constantly. When boiling hard, add sugar all at once and bring again to a full rolling boil and boil hard for **one minute,** stirring constantly. Remove from heat, add nuts and skim off any foam with metal spoon. Stir and skim for about five minutes. Ladle into glasses. Cover with ⅛ inch hot parraffin and seal. Makes 11 medium glasses.

Up in Johnny Appleseed Country, Au Glaize Village, Ohio, there is a recipe for apple butter which has won recognition for several years. We came by it from a friend and think "Appleseed Country Folds" would be glad we passed it along to you!

APPLE BUTTER

1 gallon apple cider
4 quarts peeled, cored and sliced
    apples (about 7 lbs.)
1 lb. granulated sugar
1 cup dark brown sugar
1 tablespoon ground cinnamon
1 teaspoon ground cloves
1 teaspoon ground allspice

Pour the apple cider into a large heavy enamel kettle (about a four gallon size). Bring to a boil and boil, uncovered, until volume is reduced by half. Add the apples, a few at a time, stirring all the time. Boil, uncovered, until all pieces of apple disappear and mixture is thick and glossy. Please, stir **constantly,** so mixture won't stick. Stir in the sugars, cinnamon, cloves and allspice. Remove apple butter from fire and continue to stir until all sugar is completely dissolved. Ladle hot into sterilized, pint-size jars. Fill to within ⅛ inch of the top. Seal and process for 10 minutes in a simmering hot water bath. Then store on a cool, dry shelf! Sounds good.

Strawberries! Nothing like them, picked fresh and eaten on the spot! Enjoy them to the fullest while in their short season! But then . . . . for the days ahead make some up into

STRAWBERRY PRESERVES

1 quart fresh ripe strawberries
    (may leave them whole or
    slice them)
4 cups sugar
⅓ cup water
1 tablespoon vinegar

Mix sugar, water and vinegar. Cook until sugar is dissolved. Bring to a hard boil. Add berries. Cook about 20 minutes. Set off heat and let cool before putting into jars. Place by spoonfuls into sterilized glasses and cover with ⅛ inch hot paraffin. Seal and store on pantry shelf.

An old fashioned recipe that bears handing down from generation to generation. . . .

OLD FASHIONED FIG PRESERVES

Weigh your figs and then **weigh an equal amount of sugar.** Add ¾ cup water for each pound of sugar. Boil sugar and water for about 20 minutes (makes a syrup) skim often! Add figs which you have peeled (begin at stem end!). Boil rapidly. When you have boiled for 10 minutes, add 2 lemons which you have very thinly sliced. Bring to a boil again and boil until figs are transparent and syrup thick. Remove from heat and place in shallow pans and allow to stand until syrup is as thick as honey. Then bring fruit and syrup back to a boil and pack in hot sterilized jars and seal.

The jelly jar can also hold some of the most delicious jams and sweet relishes. . . . like this recipe for

CRANBERRY CHUTNEY

1 pound cranberries
1 lemon
1 cup brown sugar
1 cup water
½ cup raisins
½ cup vinegar
1 medium onion, chopped
1 teaspoon salt
1 teaspoon dry mustard
¼ teaspoon cayenne

Peel lemon with thin peel, sliver, mix all the ingredients (including the juice from the lemon). Cook in heavy saucepan over medium heat. Stir frequently until mixture begins to thicken and the cranberries are tender. Remove from heat and stir in ½ cup ginger preserves or ⅓ cup finely chopped crystalized ginger. Cool in sterlized jars (for storing). Cover with ¼ inch paraffin and when it is set. . . . place lid on tightly. (May be stored in refrigerator without paraffin).

CRANBERRY ORANGE CHUTNEY

1 orange
2 cups raw cranberries
½ cup sugar
1 tablespoon tarragon vinegar
1 teaspoon chopped fresh mint

Remove the rind and the white membrane from the orange. Run through food chopper with the cranberries (use rind and fruit of orange). Use fine blade on chopper. Mix the fruit with the sugar, vinegar and mint. Let stand until sugar is completely dissolved. Chill for 24 hours and serve. Great with meats!

The Bread Box

Bread. . . . has been the symbol of goodness, warmth and security since long before Biblical times. We couldn't relate here just who first made bread but it is known that the Swiss Lake Dwellers crushed barley and wheat in a crude mortar. . . . that ancient Egyptians were said to knead bread with their feet. . . . and that the Chinese made bread from wheat. . . . and it is also said that the Greeks many years later set up public ovens for everybody's use. . . . and that yeast is the oldest and still the newest means of making bread rise. It makes it light and delicious! From the Bible this quotation. . . . "Know ye not that a little leaven leaveneth the whole lump. . . ."

So. . . . a little good yeast and other equally as good ingredients. . . . with a good recipe and a little practice. . . . will make you the proud baker of bread "like mama used to bake". . . .

Mix, beat, stir and knead as your recipe dictates. . . . bake at the suggested temperature in the right size pans. . . . and when the baking time is up. . . . remove from pan. . . . tap the bottom and sides. . . . if it sounds hollow. . . . it is done!

Try this first recipe for a really delicious loaf of homemade bread that will leave a mouth-watering memory with all who eat it. . . .

BREAD LIKE MAMA USED TO BAKE

1 cup warm water (in which you
    have cooked the potatoes)
2 packages dry yeast
¾ cup warm milk
½ cup sugar
¼ cup warm mashed potatoes
6-7 cups unsifted flour
2 teaspoons salt
2 eggs, beaten
¼ cup melted butter (cooled)

Measure potato water into large mixing bowl and sprinkle with the yeast. Stir until yeast is dissolved. Add milk, sugar, mashed potatoes and 2 cups flour. Beat until smooth. Cover and let rise until bubbly. Stir down and add salt and 1 cup flour. Beat until smooth. Stir in beaten eggs and butter. Add enough additional flour to make a stiff dough. Turn out onto floured board and knead until smooth and elastic (about 10 minutes). Place in a greased bowl, turning several times to grease all over dough. Cover bowl and let rise in a warm place until double in bulk (from 40-50 minutes). Punch dough down and turn out on lightly floured board. Knead lightly and divide into halves. Cover and let rest for 5 minutes. Grease 2 9x5x3 inch loaf pans. Place one half dough in each and let rise until double in size (takes about 40-50 minutes). Bake at 350° for 45 minutes or until golden brown. Remove from pans and cook before storing.

Note: It is important to keep dough out of drafts when it is rising!

MAMAW JOHNSON'S OLD FASHIONED BISCUITS

2 cups flour
2 teaspoons baking powder
1 teaspoon salt
¼ teaspoon soda
2 tablespoons shortening
¾ cup buttermilk

Sift together flour, baking powder, salt and soda. Mix in shortening. Add milk and work together. Pinch off small pieces of dough and roll into ball shape. Pat out on lightly greased and floured baking pan. Bake in hot oven, 450°, until golden brown.

You'll want to bake these mouth watering biscuits over and over again.... they're light, lovely and luscious!

WHIPPED CREAM BISCUITS

2 cups all purpose flour
3 teaspoons baking powder
¾ teaspoon salt
1 cup heavy cream which has
     been stiffly whipped

Sift flour, baking powder and salt into bowl. Mix in whipped cream with a fork. Turn batter out on lightly floured board and knead for about one minute. Pat the dough out to about ½ inch thick. Cut out biscuits with a 2-inch cutter. Place on baking sheet which has been **very** lightly greased.... and bake in a 425° oven for about 10-12 minutes or until light brown.

BUTTERMILK BISCUITS

2 cups cake flour or 1¾ cups all
     purpose flour, sifted
1 teaspoon salt
3 teaspoons baking powder
1 teaspoon sugar
½ teaspoon soda
5 tablespoons butter
⅔-¾ cup buttermilk

Always sift the flour before measuring, then add other dry ingredients, sifting again. Cut in butter. Add milk to form a soft dough. Pat out on a floured board to ½-inch thickness. Cut out biscuits, place on ungreased baking sheet. Bake 12-15 minutes at 450°. Makes 2 dozen very tender 1½-inch biscuits.

SOUR CREAM BISCUITS

2 cups enriched self-rising flour
     (spoon flour into dry
     measuring cup; level. Don't
     scoop)
1 cup dairy sour cream at room
     temperature
1 teaspoon water or milk, opt.

Blend sour cream into flour to make a soft dough. If necessary, add about 1 teaspoon water or milk. Turn out onto lightly floured surface and knead gently about 30 seconds. Roll out to ½-inch thick. Cut with floured biscuit cutter. Place on ungreased baking sheet. Bake in pre-heated, 450°, oven 10-15 minutes or until lightly browned.

'Til you've tried my favorite recipe for corn bread, don't say you "don't like cornbread".

CORN BREAD

1 package yeast
¼ cup warm water
2 cups milk, scalded
⅓ cup sugar
⅓ cup shortening or cooking oil
1 teaspoon salt
3 cups sifted all purpose flour
1 cup yellow corn meal
2 eggs, well beaten
4 cups sifted all purpose flour

Sprinkle yeast into the very warm (but not hot!) water. Stir until dissolved. In large mixing bowl, combine milk, sugar, shortening and salt. Stir in 3 cups flour until blended. Now, add well beaten eggs, yeast and corn meal. Gradually stir in 4 cups flour. On lightly floured board, using remaining flour, knead corn meal dough for 10 minutes. It should be smooth and elastic. Place cornbread dough in large, greased bowl, turning it to grease all sides dough. Cover with a towel and let rise until doubled in size. . . about 1½ hours. Turn dough onto a lightly floured surface and knead 2 minutes, then shape into loaf and turn into well greased 9½x5½x2½ loaf pan. (Place dough in pan seam side down). Let bread rise for 20 minutes in a warm place. Bake at 375° for 35-40 minutes. Turn out on side on wire rack to cool.

There's never been a better bread than this "ole time" corn bread.

BUTTERMILK CORN BREAD

1 cup sifted cornmeal
½ cup plain flour
½ teaspoon salt
½ teaspoon soda
1 egg, beaten
1 cup buttermilk
2 tablespoons shortening or butter, melted

Sift all dry ingredients and add egg and buttermilk a little at a time. Mix thoroughly. Add shortening while it is hot. Mix and pour into greased baking pan. Bake at 450° about 25 minutes or until golden brown.

Think of this with garden vegetables and cold buttermilk!

CORN MUFFINS

2 cups enriched self-rising corn
    meal
2 tablespoons sugar
2 eggs, well beaten
3/4-1 cup milk
1/4 cup oil

Stir together corn meal and sugar. Blend together: eggs, 3/4 cup milk, and oil. Add liquid all at once to corn meal mixture, stirring until smooth. If necessary, add more milk to make a medium thick batter. Fill muffin cups 2/3 full. Bake in preheated 425° oven 20-25 minutes, or until golden brown. Remove from tin onto a wire rack and cool thoroughly. Serve with butter. Makes 12 muffins.

GEORGIA HUSH PUPPIES

2 cups enriched self-rising corn
    meal
1/2 cup finely chopped onion
1 1/2-2 cups boiling water
1 egg, beaten
vegetable oil for deep frying

Combine corn meal and onion. Stir in 1 1/2 cups water, mixing until well blended. Stir in egg. Add more water, if necessary, to make a thick batter. Drop by rounded teaspoonfuls into 2-3 inches preheated 375° oil and fry until golden brown. . . .3-4 minutes, turning once. Drain on absorbent paper. Serve hot. Makes 2 dozen hush puppies.

Larry Fair, another well known "chef" shares this. . . .

MAMA'S CRACKLIN' BREAD

1 1/2 cups white cornmeal
1 1/2 cups buttermilk
1 egg
1 teaspoon salt
1 teaspoon baking powder
1 cup cracklins'

Preheat oven to 450°. Mix all dry ingredients and stir in cracklins'. Beat egg and add to buttermilk. Combine with dry ingredients and cracklins. Grease and preheat a heavy iron skillet or casserole. Pour in batter and bake for 20 minutes or 'til it springs back at the touch.

The makers of Fleischman's Yeast passed along this recipe several years ago. It deserves preserving and using often. . . .

RICH OLD FASHIONED YEAST EGG BREAD

½ cup lukewarm water
2 packages yeast
1½ cup milk (scalded)
¼ cup sugar
1 tablespoon salt
½ cup soft butter
3 eggs
6½ cups sifted flour

Dissolve yeast in water. Add sugar, salt and butter to scalded milk. Cool until lukewarm. Add beaten eggs. Combine with yeast mixture. Blend in about 4 cups of the sifted flour. Beat until smooth. Place in a well buttered bowl, turning once to coat with butter. Cover and let rise in a warm place until doubled in size. Turn out on lightly floured board and work in remaining flour. Divide into three equal parts and place in well greased 9"x5" size pans. Brush with a mixture of 2 tablespoons water and one beaten egg yolk. Let rise until dough reaches almost to the top of pans. Bake 45-50 minutes in 375° oven. The egg yolk will cause bread to have a rich brown crust. Turn out on wire rack to cool.

You'll love this Early American recipe for. . . .

MOLASSES BREAD

2½ cups flour
1 teaspoon soda
2 teaspoons baking powder
⅔ cup buttermilk
1 egg
¼ cup sugar
½ cup molasses
¼ cup melted butter

Beat egg until light and fluffy. Add sugar, molasses and butter. Add sifted dry ingredients to egg mixture alternately with buttermilk. Grease loaf pan. Pour in batter and bake at 350° one hour or until straw inserted in center comes out dry.

Expect our grandmothers always dissolved the yeast or made their own liquid yeast....but it took the oldest name in yeast history.... Fleischman ....to come up with the rapid mix method which does away with dissolving the yeast in water....and this particular recipe requires no kneading....try this one....it takes just about an hour before baking.

CRUMB COFFEE CAKE

5 tablespoons margarine, softened
⅓ cup sugar
3 egg yolks, at room
    temperature
1 cup unsifted flour
2 teaspoons ground cinnamon
2-2½ cups unsifted flour
¼ cup sugar
¼ teaspoon salt
1 pkg. active dry yeast
½ cup milk
¼ cup water
½ cup (1 stick) margarine

Cream 5 tablespoons softened margarine. Gradually beat in ⅓ cup sugar. Blend in 1 egg yolk, 1 cup flour and cinnamon. Set aside for topping.

In a large bowl, thoroughly mix ½ cup flour, remaining ¼ cup sugar, salt and undissolved active dry yeast. Combine milk, water and remaining ½ cup margarine. Heat over low heat until liquids are very warm (125°-135°). Margarine does not need to melt. Gradually add to dry ingredients and beat 2 minutes at medium speed on electric mixer, scraping bowl occasionally. Add remaining egg yolks and 1 cup additioinal flour, or enough flour to make a thick batter. Beat at high speed 2 minutes, scraping bowl occasionally. Stir in enough additional flour to make a stiff batter. Spread mixture into a well-greased 9-inch square pan. Crumble topping mixture over top of batter. Cover; let rise in a warm place, free from draft, until almost doubled in bulk, about 1 hour. Bake in 350° oven for 45 minutes, or until done. Remove from pan and cool on wire rack. If desired, drizzle with confectioners' sugar frosting. Makes one 9-inch cake.

From the Cake Tin

From the Cake Tin....

"Let 'em eat cake"! Fruit Cake, Pound Cake, Tea Cakes, Sponge Cakes....any kind of cake....but serve them **good** cake!

A word about cake baking:
Before you start.....read the recipe carefully and be sure you understand the terms....cream, beat, stir, fold, it makes a difference in the end results!
Preheat oven **before** starting....at the specified temperature....temperatures must be correct and remember.... "the oven can wait for the cake....but the cake should never wait for the oven".
Measure accurately: use size pans called for in recipe; sift flour and have it ready for measuring; chop nuts and fruits ahead of mixing time;test for doneness, insert cake tester, wooden toothpick or straw into center of cake....if it comes out clean, cake is done; cool cake before frosting.

One of the best for the Cake Tin!

BROWN SUGAR POUND CAKE

1 cup butter
½ cup Crisco
1 box light brown sugar
1 cup white sugar
5 eggs
3 cups all purpose flour, sifted
1 teaspoon baking powder
⅛ teaspoon salt
2 teaspoons vanilla
1½ cups chopped nuts
1 cup milk

Frosting:
1 cup powdered sugar
3 tablespoons butter

Cream butter, Crisco and add sugar, beating all the time. Add eggs, one at a time. Sift flour, baking powder and salt and add alternately with milk. Add vanilla and chopped nuts. Bake in a well greased and floured bundt pan for one hour or until done (test by sticking straw or toothpick into center of cake). Turn out and cool. While still slightly warm mix the following and spoon over cake:

Mix thoroughly. You may need to add a slight bit of hot water to make it thin enough to spoon over cake. You also may want to add a few chopped pecans for garnish.

Its doubtful that our ancestors thought about using zucchini in a cake, but some years ago someone tried it and the result is "mouth-watering"!

ZUCCHINI CAKE

3 eggs
1 cup salad oil (Wesson is fine)
1 teaspoon salt
3 cups flour
2 cups sugar
2 cups grated unpeeled zucchini
    squash
3 teaspoons cinnamon
1 cup chopped walnuts or pecans
3 teaspoons vanilla
3 teaspoons baking powder

Beat eggs, add sugar, oil and zucchini. Sift dry ingredients and add to egg mixture. Add vanilla and nuts. Pour into **well** greased and floured pan (9x13x2). Bake at 350° for one hour. (If using glass pan, bake at 320°).

Note: do not peel zucchini. . . . do not drain liquid when grated. . . . do not use seeds!

May be frosted with a light lemon-butter frosting if desired. However it is delicious without any trimmings.

The Milky Way Candy bar has been around for a long time . . . . and probably was never intended to be made up in a cake . . . . but somebody tried it . . . . we hope you will!

MILKY WAY CAKE

8 regular size Milky Way candy
   bars
2 sticks oleo
2 cups sugar
2½ cups flour
½ teaspoon soda
1¼ cups buttermilk
4 eggs
1 cup chopped pecans

Grease and flour tube pan. Melt Milky Way bars and one stick oleo. Set aside. Cream sugar and one stick oleo. Add eggs, one at a time. Mix soda with buttermilk. Add alternately with the flour. Add melted candy and oleo mixture. Add pecans. Bake at 325° for one hour and 10 minutes.

Frost with the following when cool:
1 cup evaporated milk
6 oz. semi-sweet chocolate chips
1 cup marshmallow cream
1 stick oleo

Cook sugar and milk to a soft ball stage. Add chocolate chips, marshmallow cream and oleo. Stir until all melted. Spread over cake. Mmmmmmmmm good.

We found this recipe in an old cookbook . . . . and it was called:

OLD TIMEY SEED CAKE

3 cups flour
1 cup milk, add ½ cup poppy
   seed to milk and let set about
   3 hours
3 cups sugar
1½ cups butter
1 teaspoon salt
5 large eggs
1 teaspoon lemon extract
1 teaspoon almond extract

Sift flour with salt. Cream butter until fluffy. Add sugar slowly. Add 1 egg. Beat well. Add a little flour, then a little milk. Beat well. Repeat this procedure until you have used all the eggs and dry ingredients and milk, blend well. Pour into a greased and lightly floured tube pan, place in unheated oven and set dial at 325°. Bake 1½ hours.

As long as we can remember....Mama....Grandma....Great Grandma....all made the traditional

STACK CAKE

1 cup butter
1 cup sugar
1 cup molasses
1 teaspoon soda
3 eggs
1 cup milk
4 cups flour
1 teaspoon salt

Cream butter and sugar. Cream well and then add molasses. Add beaten eggs. Beat well. Add milk alternately with sifted dry ingredients. Mix well. Grease and lightly flour 6 layer pans. Divide batter between pans and bake at 375° for 20 minutes. Cool on cake racks. Put together with cooked dried apples (add sugar to taste) or applesauce. No frosting....just put aside to set.

HONEY CAKE

12 tablespoons vegetable oil, plus
    2 tablespoons for preparing
    baking dish
1 cup granulated sugar
1 tablespoon baking powder
2 cups all purpose flour
8 oz. ground walnuts or pecans
1 cup raisins
3 eggs
1 (16 oz.) jar honey
1 tablespoon grated lemon rind
4 tablespoons lemon juice
¾ cup strong coffee, cooled

Preheat oven to 350°. Grease 2 8½x4½x2½ heat resistant glass baking dishes, using 1 tablespoon oil. Line with wax paper and grease again with second tablespoon of oil.
Sift together: flour, baking powder, and sugar into a large bowl. Blend in nuts and raisins. In another large bowl, mix eggs, honey, grated lemon rind, lemon juice, remaining oil and cooled coffee. With a large wooden spoon, stir the flour mixture into the honey mixture until all ingredients are well blended. Divide the batter evenly into the two prepared baking dishes. Bake 30-40 minutes or until the cakes are dark brown.

OLD FASHIONED POUND CAKE

2 sticks butter
1¾ cups sugar
6 eggs
2 cups flour
1 teaspoon vanilla
1 teaspoon baking powder
⅓ teaspoon mace
⅛ teaspoon salt

Cream butter and sugar well. Sift flour, baking powder together. Add alternately with eggs, adding one egg at a time. Beat well after each addition. Add vanilla. Bake at 325° for one hour and twenty five minutes in greased and floured tube pan.

GLAZED CARROT CAKE

2 cups unsifted all purpose flour
1⅓ cups sugar
2 teaspoons cinnamon
1 teaspoon baking soda
½ teaspoon salt
3 eggs
¾ cup buttermilk
½ cup oil
2 teaspoons vanilla
2 cups coarsely grated carrots
1 cup coarsely chopped walnuts
    lightly toasted
1 cup flaked coconut
1 8-oz. can crushed pineapple,
    drained

Preheat oven to 350°. Grease and flour a 9x13 baking pan. Combine first five ingredients. Mix well. In separate mixing bowl, beat eggs, buttermilk, oil and vanilla. Add flour mixture and blend until smooth. Fold in carrots, nuts, coconut and pineapple. Pour into pan and bake 45 minutes or until center will spring back when lightly touched and cake has pulled slightly away from edges of pan. Remove from oven immediately and poke holes every 2 inches over top with fork. Slowly pour half of hot glaze over top. When it is absorbed, add remaining glaze. Cool in pan, then cut into bars.

BUTTERMILK GLAZE
for Carrot Cake

⅔ cup sugar
⅓ cup buttermilk
⅓ cup butter
2 tablespoons light corn syrup
¼ teaspoon baking soda
1 teaspoon vanilla

Combine all ingredients except vanilla in small saucepan and bring to a boil over medium heat. Stir constantly. Reduce heat and simmer gently for five minutes. Remove from heat and stir in vanilla.

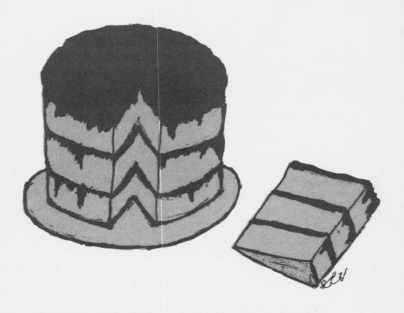

ELAINE'S FAVORITE....POPPY SEED CAKE

1 cup butter
6 eggs, separated
2½ cups sugar
1 cup buttermilk
¼ cup sweet milk
1 teaspoon almond extract
1 teaspoon lemon extract
¼ teaspoon soda
3 cups sifted flour
1 teaspoon baking powder
1 tablespoon poppy seed

Soak poppy seed in ¼ cup sweet milk. Beat egg whites until stiff. Set aside. Cream together egg yolks, butter and sugar. Cream until fluffy. Combine buttermilk with poppy seed mixture. Add almond and lemon extract and then add baking soda. Sift flour with baking powder. Add to creamed mixture alternately with buttermilk mixture. Fold in egg whites. Pour into well greased and floured 10 inch tube pan. Bake at 350° about 1 hour and 15 minutes. Remove from oven and cool 5 minutes. Remove from pan and pour orange glaze over top.

ORANGE GLAZE

1½ cups powdered sugar
1 teaspoon almond extract
½ cup orange juice

Blend until smooth and pour over warm cake.

Back in the 1800's no cake box would have been without a Chocolate Potato Cake.... especially when company was expected.... friends at Westville, Georgia.... where it is always 1850.... share this favorite recipe with us....

CHOCOLATE POTATO CAKE

½ cup real butter
1½ cups sugar
2 cups all purpose flour
2 teaspoons baking powder
1 teaspoon cinnamon
½ teaspoon nutmeg
¾ cup sweet milk
1 cup chopped nuts
½ cup raisins
1 cup mashed potatoes
½ cup melted unsweetened
   chocolate

Cream butter and sugar until fluffy. Sift dry ingredients three times. Add dry ingredients to creamed mixture. Alternate with milk. Add nuts and raisins after you have mixed them with the mashed potatoes and melted chocolate. Blend well. Grease two lined 8"x8" pans with butter and flour lightly. Bake for 35 minutes in 350° oven. This cake may be put together with chocolate fudge frosting or dust each layer with powdered sugar and cut into squares.

CHOCOLATE FUDGE FROSTING

2 1-oz. squares unsweetened
   chocolate, melted, (or *4
   tablespoons cocoa)
3 cups sugar
3 tablespoons light corn syrup
¼ teaspoon salt
1 cup milk
¼ cup butter
1 teaspoon vanilla

Combine melted chocolate, sugar, syrup, salt and milk. Cook over low heat, stirring until sugar dissolves. Cook to soft ball stage. Remove from heat; add butter and cool until just warm. Add vanilla and beat until spreading consistency. Frost lightly between layers and top and sides of cake. *If using cocoa, mix with sugar before adding rest of ingredients.

HICKORY NUT CAKE

1 cup butter
2 cups sugar
3½ cups all purpose flour
1 cup milk
3 teaspoons baking powder
5 egg whites, beaten stiff but not dry
1 pint hickory nuts, mixed with part of flour

Cream butter; gradually add sugar and blend well. Sift flour, measure, then sift again with the baking powder. Mix nuts with some of the flour. Preheat oven to 350° and grease 2 (9-inch) pans. Add flour and milk alternately to the creamed mixture. Fold in egg whites, beaten stiff, but not dry. Pour into the pans, and bake 25-30 minutes. This makes a large cake.

Another candy bar cake you'll want to share with the neighbors and you may want to keep one in the freezer for unexpected company. It's a winner!

HERSHEY BAR CAKE

½ pound real butter
2 cups sugar
4 eggs
2 teaspoons vanilla
½ teaspoon salt
½ cup chopped pecans
8 large Hershey bars
2 tablespoons water
2½ cups sifted cake flour
1 cup buttermilk
¼ teaspoon soda

Cream butter and sugar. Add and beat eggs one at a time into the mixture. Melt the Hershey bars in a double boiler with the 2 tablespoons water. Add the vanilla and salt to melted bars. Blend into the butter-sugar mixture. Mix the soda with the buttermilk and add alternately with the flour to creamed chocolate mixture. Fold in the nuts. Bake in a well greased and floured tube pan for 1½ hours. Bake at 325°. Cool and turn out on rack. Sift powdered sugar over cake.

ROZELL'S FAVORITE WHITE CAKE WITH 7 MINUTE FROSTING

2¾ cups sifted cake flour
4½ teaspoons baking powder
1 teaspoon salt
1¾ cups sugar
⅔ cups Crisco
¾ cup milk
1 teaspoon grated orange peel
1 teaspoon grated lemon peel
1 teaspoon vanilla
1 teaspoon almond extract
5 egg whites

Preheat oven to 350°. Grease and flour 3 (8x1½) layer pans (or you may want to just make two layers, if so grease and flour 2, 9x1½ inch pans). Sift flour and sugar, baking powder and salt together. Cream shortening and add flour mixture alternately with the milk. Beat until all ingredients are well blended. Add lemon and orange peel and extracts. Add egg whites about half at a time. Beat well after each addition. (Be sure egg whites are blended in well!) Divide into prepared pans and bake 30-35 minutes or until straw inserted in center comes out clean. Cool on rack and put together with:

7 MINUTE FROSTING and GINGER ORANGE FILLING for White Cake

3 egg whites
1 cup sugar
⅓ cup white Karo Syrup
3 tablespoons water
⅛ teaspoon salt
¼ teaspoon cream of tartar
1 teaspoon orange or lemon extract
1 tablespoon finely chopped
    candied ginger
3 tablespoons orange marmalade

Blend egg whites, sugar, corn syrup, water, salt and cream of tartar in top of double boiler. Place over rapidly boiling water and beat with rotary beater until mixture stands in stiff peaks. Stir in the extract.
Remove 1 cup of the frosting and place in small bowl. Fold in the ginger and orange marmalade. Spread between the cake layers. Use remaining frosting to frost sides and top of cake . . . . absolutely the most delicious white cake you ever tasted!

The Pie Safe

THE PIE SAFE

One of my earliest childhood memories is that of the Pie Safe in my Uncle's home down on the farm! When we'd be invited for Sunday dinner . . . . that's the first place I'd want to look, to see what kind of pies (and there was always more than one kind!) we'd be enjoying for dessert! They'd be baked the day before and placed in the safe away from any inquiring fly and of course to keep them in a cool place. I can vividly recall the doors on the safe . . . . made of tin with multi-circular designs perforated in the center of each door . . . . and smaller ones all around . . . . to let the air inside.

If you're lucky enough to own one . . . you know you have a treasure, or maybe you'd be lucky enough to find one in an antique store one day. Get it if you do, they make grand conversation pieces and serve beautifully as a storage area for quilts, placemats or any kind of linens. But as for me, I'd love to have one to use just as it was originally intended . . . and I'd fill it with some of the delicious pies you'll find in the PIE SAFE section of this cookbook!

Not....a pie....but Apple Brown Betty....just has to be one of the best old fashioned desserts of all time....try this recipe for "seconds"!

APPLE BROWN BETTY

2 cups coarse dry bread crumbs
   (home made-not canned)
5 tablespoons melted butter
5 cups cored, pared tart apples
½ cup brown sugar (packed)
1½ tablespoons lemon juice
1 teaspoon grated lemon peel
½ teaspoon ground cinnamon
⅓ cup hot water
1 cup whipping cream
1 teaspoon sugar

Heat oven to 350°. Mix crumbs and butter in small bowl. Combine apples, brown sugar, lemon juice, peel and cinnamon in large bowl. Spread one third of the crumb mixture in bottom of greased 1½ quart baking dish. Top crumbs with half the apple mixture. Repeat layers. Top with remaining crumbs. Add water. Bake covered 25 minutes. Remove cover and bake until apples are tender and top is golden brown and crunchy. Takes about 20-25 minutes. Cook until slightly warm. Whip the cream with the tablespoon sugar until it forms soft peaks. Serve over top of Apple Brown Betty.

One of the best pecan pies you'll ever eat!

SOUTHERN PECAN PIE WITH AN ORANGE FLAVOR

3 eggs
¾ cup brown sugar
½ cup dark syrup
½ cup orange juice
1 teaspoon grated lemon peel
½ teaspoon vanilla extract
1 cup pecans (broken into
   medium pieces)
1 unbaked pie crust (9 inch)
¼ cup melted butter
dash of salt

Beat eggs thoroughly. Add sugar, syrup and salt. Mix well. Add grated lemon peel, orange juice, vanilla and butter. Put pecans in pie shell and pour mixture over. Bake at 350° for 35-45 minutes. Cool before serving. May be served with whipped cream.

OLD FASHIONED COCONUT PIE

1 cup fresh grated coconut (or
  Angel Flake Coconut)
1 cup milk
1 tablespoon flour
3 eggs, beaten
1 cup sugar
⅛ teaspoon salt
½ stick butter, melted and
  browned slightly

Make your pie crust from your favorite recipe (or use a frozen one from the dairy case); 9 inch crust. Mix coconut and milk. Mix sugar and flour and salt. Blend into milk mixture. Add beaten eggs and butter. Pour into uncooked pie shell and dust nutmeg over the top. Bake at 350° until set (insert knife in center of pie to see if set), unsually takes about 30 minutes. Cool and you may want to serve with fresh whipped cream on top. Sprinkle with a little more coconut which you have lightly toasted.

Fondest memories of childhood days. . . .was a piece of homemade chocolate pie after school. . . .this comes as near being what I remember. . . .and you'll do well to try it, if you like chocolate pie.

MRS. EDITH BEAN'S CHOCOLATE PIE

1¼ cups sugar
4 tablespoons cocoa
¼ cup flour
2 cups milk
3 eggs separated
½ stick real butter
⅛ teaspoon salt
1 teaspoon vanilla
1 (9") baked pie shell
6 tablespoons sugar

Mix sugar, cocoa and flour together. Add enough of the milk to make a thick paste. Beat in the egg yolks. . . .mix well. Heat the remaining milk with the butter and salt. Add this mixture to the first and cook over medium heat until thick. Stir often to prevent sticking or burning. Remove from heat and add vanilla. Cool and pour into baked shell. Make a meringue with the egg whites, beat until stiff adding about 6 tablespoons of sugar as you beat. Spread over pie and place in 375° oven until golden brown.

If you like cobblers, maybe this cherry cobbler will become your best "company" dessert. . . . men especially like it.

CHERRY COBBLER

2 cups cooked, tart cherries, drain
    off juice
1/2 cup cherry juice
1 cup sugar
1 cup flour
1/2 cup sugar (extra)
2 teaspoons baking powder
1/2 teaspoon salt
1/2 cup milk
1/2 stick butter

Heat the cherries, juice and one cup sugar to the boiling point. Combine the flour, the 1/2 cup sugar, baking powder, salt and milk. Melt the butter in a baking dish. Pour in the batter. Spread over bottom of dish and then pour the cherry mixture over (have the cherry mixture very hot before pouring into batter). Bake in 375° oven until golden brown 20-25 minutes. Delicious topped with a scoop of vanilla ice cream or another "dab" of butter!

Rich, sunshine sweet strawberries. . . . select the smaller ones. . . . they're the best and so much sweeter! Then follow these directions:

FRESH STRAWBERRY PIE

1 quart strawberries
3 tablespoons cornstarch
1 cup sugar
1/4 teaspoon almond extract
1 baked 9-inch pie shell

Arrange half the berries, uncooked, large end down in precooked shell. Prepare remaining berries with sugar, cornstarch and extract, mashing berries to make their own juice. Cook until thick over low heat. Cool. Pour into shell over the whole berries. Serve cold with whipped sweet cream.

Worthy of seconds!

BUTTERMILK PIE

3 eggs
1/2 cup self-rising flour
1 stick butter
1/2 teaspoon salt
2 cups sugar
1/2 teaspoon soda
2 cups buttermilk
1 tablespoon vanilla
2 unbaked pie shells

Sift sugar, flour and salt together. Add eggs and melted butter. Dissolve the soda in buttermilk and add flour mixture. Beat well and pour into shells. Bake 15 minutes at 400° and then reduce to 350° and cook for 25-30 minutes longer. Insert knife in center to see if firm.

Peach season in Georgia brings out "the best" in peach recipes and this is at the top of the pie list.

"BEST COMPANY" PEACH PIE

5 cups sliced ripe peaches (not mushy ripe)
3 tablespoons Brandy
1/2 small carton sour cream
3/4 cup brown sugar
Crust:
1/2 cup brown sugar
1/2 cup white sugar
1 cup flour
1/3 cup butter

Place peach slices in bowl and sprinkle with the Brandy. Set aside.
Crust: Mix flour and sugar and then cream with butter. Press into 9-inch pie plate (deep dish plate). Bake in 400° oven for 5 minutes. Reduce heat to 325° and bake 10 minutes longer. . . . until done. Fill cooled crust with the peach and Brandy mixture. Cover lightly with sour cream and sprinkle top generously with brown sugar.

Easy to prepare and so good you'll serve it over and over again.

If you don't have those fresh apples from the orchard and you're just yearning for a good ole apple pie. . . . try this one! Probably one of the most sensational recipes around when it was first created.

MOCK APPLE PIE

2 cups water
2 teaspoons cream of tartar
1/8 teaspoon nutmeg
4 tablespoons butter
1 1/4 cups sugar
20 to 25 Ritz crackers
1/8 teaspoon cinnamon
pastry for a double crust pie

Place water, sugar, cream of tartar in saucepan. Bring to a rapid boil. Drop in the crackers, one at a time and **do not stir**. Let boil on low heat for 10 minutes. Remove from heat and pour mixture into an unbaked crust. Top with butter, cinnamon and nutmeg. Place the top crust on the pie. Bake for 12-15 minutes at 425° or until brown. Cool and serve as you would a real apple pie. Promise you'll get a great surprise, a pleasant one!

Simply scrumptious dessert! Found in an old "Kellogg" book.

FRESH PEACH CRISP

½ cup butter, softened
1 cup sugar
2 eggs
½ teaspoon nutmeg
½ teaspoon vanilla extract
1½ cups toasted bread crumbs
(small cubes)
2 cups Corn Flakes
4 cups sliced fresh peaches
1 tablespoon lemon juice

Cream butter and sugar in mixing bowl. Beat well. Add eggs and beat well again. Stir in nutmeg, vanilla, bread cubes and Corn Flakes. Spread half of the mixture in a buttered shallow baking dish (1½ quart size). Arrange peach slices evenly over top. Sprinkle with lemon juice and then spread remaining half of Corn Flake mixture on top. Bake in moderate oven (375º) about 25 minutes. Serve hot with cream.

Another good pie from the Pie Safe. . . one you'll remember as being a favorite "right next to Mincemeat Pie" at Christmas or Thanksgiving. . . .

RAISIN PIE

2 cups raisins
¼ cup lemon juice
grated rind of 1 lemon
1 cup orange juice
1 tablespoon grated orange peel
1½ cups sugar
4 tablespoons flour
⅛ teaspoon salt
1 tablespoon finely chopped
crystalized ginger

Mix lemon juice, orange juice, ginger and the grated rind with the raisins and set aside until raisins begin to absorb the liquid. Mix the sugar, flour and salt and add to raisin mixture. Cook over low heat until mixture begins to thicken. Pour into prepared pie shell and place dots of butter over filling before topping with the pie crust. Put top into place and crimp edges. Make design on top with fork so steam can escape. Bake 10 minutes and lower heat to 350º and cook for 35 minutes longer (or until top is brown).

SOUTHERN SWEET POTATO PIE

2 cups mashed cooked sweet
  potatoes (you may use
  canned, but I prefer to cook
  the fresh ones when they're
  good and "sticky")
2 eggs, beaten
¾ cup sugar
½ teaspoon salt
½ teaspoon cinnamon
½ teaspoon nutmeg
1⅓ cups milk
¼ cup rum (or I prefer Apricot
  Brandy)
¼ cup melted butter
brown sugar

Line your 9 inch pie pan with your favorite pie crust pastry. Combine all the above ingredients but the brown sugar in a large bowl. Mix well. Blend until smooth, no lumps, please. Pour into unbaked pie shell and sprinkle top with brown sugar. Bake for about 10 minutes at 425° then reduce heat to 300° and bake for about 45-50 minutes more, or until knife inserted in center comes out clean and filling is firm. If crust has a tendency to get too brown, fold aluminum foil around the edges until pie finished cooking. Mighty good eatin'!

This one makes its own crust and is a special favorite of Jane Brewer of the Alabama Poultry and Egg Association. Thanks to her, you can make it a favorite of yours.

EGG CUSTARD PIE

3 large eggs
1 15-oz. can evaporated milk
1 cup sugar
3 tablespoons all purpose flour
3 tablespoons melted butter
nutmeg to taste

Grease and flour well, a 9-inch pie plate. Be sure all areas are well covered. Combine all the above ingredients in a blender. Blend 30 seconds (be sure eggs are blended). Pour into prepared pie plate and bake at 350° for 40-45 minutes or until knife inserted in center comes out clean. Pie will rise but will settle as it cools and will form a light crust. Serves 6-8 and is absolutely delicious. You may want to add a "dollop" of whipped cream.

CHESS PIE

3 eggs
1¼ cups sugar
¼ pound real butter
1 tablespoon flour
1 tablespoon meal
4 tablespoons grated lemon peel
½ teaspoon lemon extract
1 teaspoon vanilla extract
½ cup finely chopped pecans

Prepare pastry for two 8-inch pie pans. Cream butter with eggs and sugar. Mix flour and meal and add to egg mixture. Add extracts. Mix well with the grated lemon peel. If you are using aluminum pie pans, preheat a cookie sheet and place pans on it in order for the bottom crust to brown. In any case, aluminum or glass pie plates, be sure to put pastry shells in 350° preheated oven for about 7 minutes **before** putting in the filling (this prevents a "doughy" crust next to the filling). Pour in filling and sprinkle pecans over top. Bake for 50-60 minutes, or until knife inserted in center comes out clean.

LEMON JELLY PIE

2 cups sugar
2 tablespoons corn meal
1 tablespoon all purpose flour
4 eggs
¼ cup melted butter
¼ cup milk
¼ cup fresh lemon juice
1 tablespoon fresh grated lemon
    peel
1 9-inch unbaked pie shell

Mix sugar, corn meal and flour in large mixing bowl. Add eggs one at a time, beat well after each addition. Stir in melted butter, milk, juice and peel. Pour into unbaked pie shell. Bake in preheated oven at 350° for about 50 minutes or until set. Best served slightly warm. Tastes very much like a Chess Pie.

Our thanks to the Georgia Egg Commission for this "tasty morsel".

Doug Wallace, the South's most entertaining, most interesting and most liked weather man....on WRBL-TV....gave us his favorite Pumpkin Pie recipe. He says there's nothing like plucking your own Ala-Gold Pumpkin from "the pea patch". Cut, peel and prepare it, then make some of it up into this pie. Sit back and enjoy....

DOUG'S ALA-GOLD PIE

2 cups Ala-Gold pumpkin, cooked
    and mashed
2 eggs, slightly beaten
1 cup evaporated milk
⅔ cup sugar
1 tablespoon flour
½ teaspoon ginger
½ teaspoon nutmeg
½ teaspoon salt

Mix sugar, flour, ginger, nutmeg and salt together. Add to prepared pumpkin. Fold in eggs and add milk. Pour into 9-inch unbaked pie shell. Cook 45 minutes in 400° oven or until filling is set and crust is evenly browned.

The Cookie Jar and Sugar Spoon

COOKIE JAR AND SUGAR SPOON

Cookie Jar and Sugar Spoon: Delicious cake morsels and candies! One of childhood's favorite memories is the Cookie Jar and the delightful taste of those sometimes "forbidden" sweets. Old fashioned tea cakes, gingerbread men and raisin bars. . . . some forever memorable delights! The also "never to be forgotten" aroma which permeated the whole house when it was cookie baking day! And the candies. . . . divinity with hickory nuts. . . chocolate fudge with walnuts. . . and the taffy! Nothing has ever come up to the old fashioned "Taffy Pull". . . especially around Christmas time! Sweets for the Sweet and we hope you enjoy our selection of both cookies and candies. . . some old. . . some new.

A tasty cookie that deserves a double batch! Must have been passed along by some Irish friends because they're called

BLARNEY-STONE COOKIES

½ cup butter (softened)
¼ cup sugar
1 egg, separated
1 teaspoon vanilla
2 tablespoons milk (whole cream is better!)
2 teaspoons grated lemon peel
2 teaspoons grated orange peel
1¼ cups sifted all purpose flour
1 cup chopped nuts

Cream butter and add sugar gradually. Combine beaten egg yolk, vanilla extract, milk, grated lemon and orange peel. Add to creamed butter and sugar. Add flour (little at a time). Blend thoroughly and chill for one hour. Beat egg whites slightly. Take one teaspoonful of dough and dip one side in egg white and then in chopped nuts. Place nut side up on greased cookie sheet. Place about 2 inches apart. Bake in 325°F oven for 20 to 25 minutes or until slightly browned. Makes 2½ dozen cookies.

There's a lot to be said for the old fashioned cookie jar . . . . it didn't always hold a variety of cookies . . . . but one you would always find . . . . old fashioned sugar cookies . . . . and when they were being baked . . . . you could hardly wait . . . . and what a wonderful thing to "snitch" when Mama wasn't looking . . . . they're just as good today . . . .

OLD FASHIONED COOKIES

1 cup sugar
½ teaspoon salt
¼ cup soft butter
1 egg
1 teaspoon grated lemon peel
1 teaspoon vanilla
3 cups sifted all-purpose flour
1 teaspoon baking powder
1 egg white slightly beaten

Cream sugar, salt and butter. Beat egg, lemon rind and extract into creamed mixture. Beat until fluffy. Sift flour and baking powder. Stir gradually into creamed ingredients. Roll dough ⅛" thick on floured board. Cut into any desired shape with the cookie cutter. Place on an ungreased cookie sheet. Bake in a moderate oven -350° - for 10 to 12 minutes or until light brown around the edges. Remove to rack to cool. Store in airtight container. Makes about 7 dozen.

A recipe which can probably be found in most good cooks kitchen.

A delightfully different
RAISIN COOKIES

½ cup butter
1¼ cups sugar
1 teaspoon vanilla
3 egg whites
1 cup flour (which has been sifted
   three times)
1 cup seedless raisins

Cream butter, sugar and vanilla until very light and fluffy. Gradually beat in egg whites, one at a time, beat well after each addition (beat for at least 1 minute each time). Add the well sifted flour alternately with the raisins. Drop by half teaspoonful onto a well buttered baking sheet. Space them 2 inches apart. Bake in 425° oven for 10-12 minutes. Delicate goodies!

Another pioneer cookbook goodie is this recipe for

RAISIN NUT BARS

1 cup flour
½ teaspoon baking powder
½ teaspoon salt
1 cup sugar
1 teaspoon cinnamon
2 eggs
1 stick butter (¼ lb.)
1 cup raisins
1 cup nuts (walnuts or pecans)

Mix all dry ingredients. Add the melted butter and beaten eggs. Add raisins and nuts. Turn into greased and very lightly floured shallow baking pan. Bake at 350°F for about 25 minutes. Cool and cut into squares or inch wide fingers.

OLD FASHIONED GINGER SNAPS

1 cup sugar
½ teaspoon salt
¾ cup butter
2 cups flour
1 egg
½ teaspoon cloves
1 teaspoon ginger
2 teaspoons soda
4 tablespoons molasses
2 teaspoons cinnamon

Cream butter and sugar. Add egg. Beat well. Add molasses to which you have added the soda. Mix cloves, ginger and cinnamon with flour. Add dry mixture a little at a time to the sugar mixture. Mix well. Drop by teaspoonful on greased cookie sheet. Bake at 375°F. for 10 minutes.

About 15 years ago this delightful recipe appeared in the pages of McCalls Magazine. Don't know who created it, but we invite you to bake these delicious

KARO LACE COOKIES

1 cup sifted flour
1 cup chopped flaked coconut
   (or nuts, or half of each)
½ cup firmly packed brown sugar
½ cup white Karo Syrup
½ cup margarine
1 teaspoon vanilla

Mix flour and coconut. Combine Karo, brown sugar and margarine in heavy saucepan. Bring to a boil over medium heat, stirring constantly. Remove from heat and gradually blend in flour mixture, then vanilla. Drop onto heavy duty foil covered cookie sheet by small teaspoonfuls, 3 inches apart. Bake in 350° oven for 8-10 minutes. Cool 3-4 minutes on wire rack until foil may be easily peeled off. Remove foil. Place cookies on rack covered with paper towel. Makes about 4 dozen cookies.

One of the best cookies ever to go in the cookie jar

MOLASSES-GINGER COOKIES

½ cup butter
1 cup molasses
2 tablespoons warm water
1 egg
4 teaspoons baking powder
3 cups flour
¼ teaspoon salt
¼ teaspoon soda
½ teaspoon ginger
1½ teaspoons cinnamon

Mix the butter, (which has been melted) molasses and warm water. Add beaten egg. Sift together all the dry ingredients. Add to first mixture to make a soft dough. Let stand about 20 minutes until dough is thickened. Roll out (a small portion at a time) on a floured board. Roll out ¼-inch thick. Cut with floured doughnut cutter. Place on well greased baking sheet. Bake at 375° for about 15 minutes. Store in a tight cookie jar. Cookies will become soft and oh so delicious! Makes 4 dozen.

I don't know where this cookie originated but you've probably tried it in various forms. I like this version of a 49'ers Gold Bar which the Domino Sugar people suggest:

49'ers GOLD BAR

1½ cups dried apricots
4 eggs
1 cup firmly packed Domino Light Brown Sugar
1 cup Domino Granulated Sugar
½ teaspoon salt
2 teaspoons grated orange peel
2 cups sifted all purpose flour
2 teaspoons double acting baking powder
½ teaspoon nutmeg
1 cup chopped walnuts
powdered sugar

Soak apricots in water until soft. Drain well and cut into small pieces. Beat eggs well. Blend sugar and salt. Gradually beat into eggs. Beat until light and foamy. Add orange peel.
Sift flour, baking powder and nutmeg. Gradually fold into egg mixture. Add apricots and nuts and mix slightly. Spread batter into 2 greased 9 inch square pans. Bake in 350° oven for 30-35 minutes or until done. When cool, cut in 1 inch by 3 inch bars. Roll in powdered sugar. Continue to cool and when absolutely cold, roll again in powdered sugar and store in airtight container. (If they last long enough to store! They're mighty good). Makes about 36 bars.

Another goodie for the cookie jar! It's a prize winner called

NUTTY FINGERS

2 cups plain flour
¾ cup butter
2 teaspoons cold water
4 tablespoons powdered sugar
1 cup finely chopped pecans
2 teaspoons vanilla

Cream butter and add sugar . . . . then water and flour, vanilla and nuts. Make dough out in rolls about the size of a large pecan and cook in a slow oven (300-325°F) until slightly brown. Do not overcook! Put one cup powdered sugar in a paper bag. After nutty fingers cool a little, put a few (maybe 6) in the bag of sugar and shake until completely covered with sugar. Repeat until all have been covered.

They're simply good! Our thanks go to an area cook who shared with us many years ago.

PECAN CLUSTERS

¼ cup butter or margarine
½ cup sugar
1 egg
½ teaspoon vanilla
1 oz. (1½ squares) unsweetened
    chocolate, melted
½ cup sifted flour
¼ teaspoon baking powder
½ teaspoon salt
2 cups pecans (broken pieces)

Cream butter and sugar; add egg, vanilla and melted chocolate. Mix well. Sift flour, baking powder and salt. Stir into creamed mixture. Add pecans. Drop by teaspoon onto greased baking sheet. Bake at 350° for 10 minutes. Makes 1½ dozen cookies. If desired ½ cup raisins may also be added at same time you add pecans. Good for the cookie jar!

This little recipe has been handed around so many times, we've no idea who originated it. . . . but is it ever good! Could have come from an old cookie jar but it certainly belongs in today's!

PECAN PUFFS

½ cup butter
4 tablespoons sugar
1 teaspoon vanilla
1 cup flour
1 cup finely chopped pecans
powdered sugar (a cup or more- 2
    cups if you double the recipe)

Cream butter and sugar and add vanilla, nuts and flour. Shape dough into small balls (about the size of a marble). Bake on an ungreased cookie sheet for about 30 minutes at 300°. Roll in powdered sugar while still hot. And roll them again after cooling. You should try this recipe exactly as stated for first pan. Cookies should be brown on bottom. Do not cook until brown on top or all over. . . . if you find the above time too long. . . .cut to 20 or 25 minutes.

APRICOT MOLASSES BARS

1 cup flour
1 teaspoon baking powder
½ teaspoon salt
¼ teaspoon baking soda
½ cup peanut butter
¼ cup softened butter or margarine
½ cup firmly packed brown sugar
  (light)
½ cup molasses
2 eggs
⅔ cup chopped dried apricots

Stir together, flour, baking powder, salt and baking soda until well mixed. Reserve. In electric mixer, cream together peanut butter, and butter until well mixed. Add sugar and molasses; cream until light and fluffy. Add eggs; beat well. Stir in dry ingredients until well mixed. Stir in apricots. Spread mixture evenly in a 9"x9" baking pan sprayed with vegetable cooking spray. Bake in 350°F oven about 30 minutes or until done. Cool on wire cake rack. Cut into 16 squares.

From a 1950's cookbook, we tried a fancy little tea cake and found it good enough to be included here. . . . it is called simply

LITTLE TEA CAKES

2 eggs, slightly beaten
1 cup brown sugar, firmly packed
½ cup all purpose flour
⅓ teaspoon salt
1 cup chopped pecans
¼ teaspoon baking powder

Beat the eggs. Sift the flour, salt and baking powder together. Add sugar to beaten eggs. Blend. Mix in the dry ingredients. Fold in pecans. Fill small greased muffin tins ⅔ full. Place a whole pecan on top each. Bake in 350° oven for 10 minutes. Let cool in tins 5 minutes. Sprinkle top with powdered sugar.

May also be baked in paper lined small muffin tins.

BASIC SPICE DOUGH

1 cup firmly packed brown sugar
1 teaspoon baking powder
½ teaspoon salt
3 teaspoons cinnamon
2 teaspoons allspice
¾ cup margarine (1½ sticks),
   softened
2 eggs
1 teaspoon vanilla
*2¼ cups all-purpose flour

Combine first 8 ingredients in large mixer bowl at low speed for 1 minutes. **Do not over mix.** Gradually add flour to above mixture at low speed until just a stiff dough forms, about 1 minute. If desired, refrigerate cookie dough roll up to 2 weeks and bake when needed. Use ⅓ of Basic Spice Dough with:

DATE STUFFED SPICE BALLS

⅓ prepared Basic Spice Dough

Slit about 18-24 pitted dates with knife or scissors and stuff with pecan half. Pinch small ball of dough (walnut size) from prepared dough; flatten with fingers; wrap around date; roll in hands to form a ball. Place balls on ungreased baking sheet; bake at 375°F for 8 to 10 minutes. (Cookies will begin to crack on top). Roll warm cookies in powdered sugar Re-roll when cool. Makes about 1 to 1½ dozen cookies.

*If using self-rising flour in Basic Spice Dough, omit baking powder and salt, and reduce margarine to ½ cup.

ROLLED BASIC DOUGH CUT-OUTS

This recipe is made from ⅓ of prepared Basic Spice Dough. Roll ⅓ prepared dough ¼ inch thick. Cut dough with cookie cutter; place on ungreased cookie sheet. Bake at 375°F. for 8-10 minutes. Decorate cooled cookies, if desired.

The Best Short Cookie you'll ever eat.

THE BEST SHORT COOKIE

1 cup butter
1 cup sugar
1 cup powdered sugar
2 eggs
1 cup salad oil
1 teaspoon salt
1 teaspoon vanilla
1 teaspoon soda
1 teaspoon cream of tartar
4 cups, 4 tablespoons flour

Cream butter, sugars and eggs. Add oil and beat well. Sift salt, cream of tartar and flour with soda and add a little at a time to the cream mixture. Add vanilla. Heat oven to 350°. Drop batter by teaspoons on ungreased sheet. Dip bottom of a glass in sugar and press each cookie (dip in sugar for each cookie). Cook 8-10 minutes. Do not overcook. Should be brown around edges. Cool on paper towels and store in air tight containers. Should be delightfully crisp and absolutely good!

Naomi Hacker....Long time home economist with the Georgia-Alabama Peanut Association shared her delicious recipe for peanut butter candy....called

BUCKEYES

1 pound butter (room temperature)
2 pounds powdered sugar
2 cups peanut butter (smooth or chunky)
12 ounces semi-sweet chocolate
½ block paraffin (2 oz.)

Mix butter, sugar and peanut butter and roll to size of buckeyes (approximately 1 inch in diameter). Chill. Melt chocolate and paraffin in double boiler. With a wooden toothpick, dip balls in chocolate mixture, leaving top uncoated for "buckeye" effect. Refrigerate until serving time. Makes about 16 dozen....and they are good! (You may want to try just half the recipe at first....but they do go fast!)

Pick a dry, clear day for this one, and get a marble slab, scissors, sauce pan and a candy thermometer.

OLD FASHIONED MINTS

2 cups sugar
½ stick butter
1 cup cold water
3 drops oil of peppermint
food coloring

Put the sugar, water and butter in a saucepan. Cover and bring to a steam. Uncover the pan and put the thermometer in boiling syrup. Bring to a 260°F temperature. Chill the marble slab by rubbing down with ice cubes. Wipe dry and grease slab thoroughly with butter. Pour hot syrup on slab. Add coloring and peppermint. Immediately fold the edges of candy to the center and when cool enough to handle, take it off the slab and with well buttered hands start to pull the candy. The more it wrinkles, the prettier the mints will be. Pull out into long ropes and cut to desired lengths with chilled scissors.

Divinity! Many recipes for this one too, but the greatest difference is in the color you make it. . . . and the amount. . . . basically. . . . divinity is divinity and our best advice comes like this: pick a nice, clear, dry day for making it or else be sure you keep mixture out of a draft. . . .

DIVINITY

2 cups sugar
1/3 cup white Karo syrup
1/2 cup water
1/8 teaspoon salt
2 egg whites
1 cup chopped pecans (or you
      may prefer to leave in halves
      and put on top of each piece
      of candy rather than mixed in)

Mix sugar, syrup, water and salt. Bring to a boil and cook until syrup reaches hard ball stage when tested in cold water (or gauged by your candy thermometer). Beat egg whites until stiff but not dry. . . . slowly pour syrup into egg whites beating constantly. (If you like. . . . 1/2 teaspoon vanilla may be added while beating). Add chopped pecans, if you desire. When mixture begins to hold its shape. . . . drop quickly by teaspoonfuls onto waxed paper.

Ask most folks about their favorite candy and it will probably be chocolate fudge! You may have your favorite recipe but we hope you'll try this unusual one for

BUTTERMILK FUDGE

2 cups sugar
2 tablespoons white corn syrup
1 teaspoon baking soda
1 cup buttermilk
1 stick butter
1 cup chopped nuts
3 tablespoons cocoa

Mix the soda with the buttermilk. Add to the sugar which you have mixed with the cocoa and placed in a large saucepan. Stir in the corn syrup. Cook over medium heat until medium hard ball forms when tested in cold water (or if you have a candy thermometer cook until it reaches 240°F). Remove from heat. Add butter and beat well. Add nuts when mixture begins to thicken. Pour into buttered pan and cool. Cut into squares.

An old fashioned recipe with a great taste!

JIFFY FUDGE

2 (3-oz.) pkgs. cream cheese
4 cups powdered sugar, sifted
2 (1-oz.) squares unsweetened
    chocolate, melted
½ teaspoon vanilla
⅛ teaspoon salt
½ cup chopped pecans

Beat cream cheese until soft and smooth. Slowly blend in sugar. Add melted chocolate. Mix well. Stir in vanilla and pecans. Press into well buttered 8x8x2 inch pan. Chill until firm. Cut into squares. Keep in cool place.

The Home Economists in the Pet Milk Kitchen passed this one along many years ago . . . . it still is a favorite.

FABULOUS FUDGE

2¼ cups sugar
¾ cup Pet Evaporated Milk
16 large marshmallows or 1 cup
    marshmallow creme
¼ cup butter
¼ teaspoon salt
1 (8-oz.) pkg. Hershey's Semi-
    Sweet Chocolate Pieces
1 teaspoon vanilla
1 cup chopped nuts

Place sugar, milk, marshmallow (or marshmallow creme), butter and salt in a heavy 2 quart saucepan. Cook over medium heat until it comes to a boil, stirring constantly. Boil and stir for five minutes. Take off heat, stir in chocolate bits and stir until they are melted. Stir in vanilla and nuts. Spread in a buttered 8 inch pan. Cool and cut into squares.

Maybe you've tried this recipe for Christmas Mounds, but if you haven't, we do suggest you try it. Easy to make and great to the taste. Another good addition to your candy recipe file.

CHRISTMAS MOUNDS

1 pkg. (6-oz.) Semi-Sweet
    Chocolate Pieces
1 pkg. (6-oz.) Caramel Chips
1 can (5½-oz.) Chowmein Noodles

Put chocolate and caramel pieces in top of double boiler and melt over hot water. Immediately stir in Chow Mein noodles, breaking them slightly with edge of spoon. Drop by teaspoonfuls onto waxed paper. Shape into little mounds and cool in refrigerator. Makes about 40 pieces.

Like Bon Bons? The Wine Institute of California shared this interesting recipe with us some years ago, and its worthy of including in this section of "Country Cookin". Country Bon Bons. . . .

RAISIN WINE BON BONS

2 cup California raisins (light or dark)
2 cups walnuts
4½ cups crushed Vanilla Wafers (that's 2 pkgs., 7¼-oz. size)
2⅓ cups sifted powdered sugar
1 tablespoon cocoa
¾ cup California Muscatel, Port or Sherry

Finely chop raisins and walnuts. Crush Vanilla Wafers into fine crumbs. Combine all ingredients mixing thoroughly with hands until well blended. Shape into small balls, about 1-inch in diameter. Store in air-tight container.

Note: Variations-Roll balls in ½ cup sifted powdered sugar mixed with 1 tablespoon cocoa. Or, roll balls in 1 teaspoon instant coffee. Or, roll balls in plain powdered sugar.

You can use the following mixture for making three different cookies, simply by substituting the liquer in each first. . . .

BOURBON BALLS

2 cups Vanilla Wafer crumbs
2 tablespoons cocoa
1½ cups powdered sugar
1 cup chopped pecans (chopped finely)
2 tablespoons white corn syrup
¼ cup Bourbon

Mix the Vanilla Wafer crumbs, 1 cup of the powdered sugar, and the pecans. Add the corn syrup and Bourbon. Mix well. Shape into 1-inch balls and roll in the remaining ½ cup powdered sugar. Pack in tightly covered tin boxes or jars. Let set overnight before serving. Makes about 3½ dozen balls depending on size.

RUM BALLS

Same as above, except substitute Rum for Bourbon.

BRANDY BALLS

Same as above, except substitute Brandy for Bourbon.

Spring House Coolers

SPRING HOUSE COOLERS

Those of us who are "thirty-nine and holding" (and older!) can for the most part readily recall a visit to Grandpa's farm (or perhaps, as in my case . . . a visit to a favorite uncle) down in the country side of Tennessee . . . . where the highlight of a visit was a trip to the Spring House! There it stood, a little wooden house astride a spring stream of the coldest water you can possibly imagine! A spring flowing right out of the ground . . . with water as clear as a crystal! And as you stepped inside you saw crock after crock with clean white cloths tied over the top and a nice heavy clean rock placed on top of the lid covering the cloth. This was sort of a "safety" measure, just in case someone or something decided to take a look inside and perhaps taste some of the goodness inside the crock. You'd have a bit of trouble getting in it . . . but, given permission, you uncovered it and were allowed to take "the dipper" and fill it to the brim . . . . with cold, cold, sweet milk, buttermilk or homemade lemonade . . . kept so deliciously cold and fresh by the bubbling spring water which sometimes came almost to the top of the crock . . . and over on one side . . . another crock which, when uncovered, displayed fresh, golden butter . . . . "little pats", half pounds and pounds . . . made even more appetizing by the flower or emblem imprint from the butter mold!

Memories one would not want to forget . . . . anymore than you'd want to forget how to make some of the delicious "Springhouse Coolers" . . . . we've gathered for you here . . . .

Long, long ago those who visited the Glenwood Plantation House down in Louisiana.... enjoyed this refreshing and (as they describe it) "altogether heavenly" tea drink....

MINT TEA DRINK

2 cups sugar
2 cups water
2 cups strong tea
2 cups crushed mint leaves
1/3 cup fresh lemon juice

You let the sugar and water come to a boil. Mix with lemon juice. Pour hot strong tea over crushed mint leaves. Let stand unti cool. Strain and pour into syrup and lemon juice mixture. Pour into glasses half filled with finely crushed ice, decorate with mint and serve at once.

Another pioneer recipe....

BLACKBERRY OR CHERRY CORDIAL

When the fruit is ripe and plentiful.... clean and boil the berries or cherries. Mash and strain.... use the following proportions:

1 cup sugar
1/2 teaspoon cinnamon
1 teaspoon cloves
1 teaspoon allspice
1 cup brandy

Add this to 4 cups juice. Boil ten minutes and cool. Add 1 cup brandy. Store in bottle or jars. Use discreetly!

The pioneers handed this one down for modern cooks.... great from the springhouse or the refrigerator.... served icy cold and generously!

STRAWBERRY SHRUB

2 cups fresh ripe strawberries
1 cup vinegar
sugar

Cover ripe berries with vinegar. Let stand for 24 hours. Then heat to boiling point. Cool and strain. To each cup of juice, add 1 cup sugar and boil for ten minutes. Store in jars with tight lid. (Suggest storing in refrigerator) When ready to serve, add 3 tablespoons of juice to a glass of crushed ice and water. Old recipe.... still good....

The spring house probably never housed this refresher, but the Apple Institute says....it would have been mighty good chilled with that cold fresh water....try it chilled in your refrigerator and believe you'll agree....it's zizzy!

CHAMPAGNE APPLE PUNCH

1 quart ice cold apple juice
1 quart ice cold ginger ale
maraschino cherries
twists of lemon peel

Combine apple juice and ginger ale. Pour into champagne glasses and place cherry and twist of lemon peel. Simple....but simply delicious!

In the good ole' summertime....what could be better than a big glass of

FRONT PORCH PUNCH

1 cup strong tea
1 cup sugar
½ cup lemon juice
½ cup orange juice
1 (32 oz.) bottle ginger ale
crushed ice

Dilute the sugar in the hot tea. Cool. Mix the fruit juices and add to cool tea mixture. Store in refrigerator until ready to serve....then add ginger ale just before serving....pour over glasses half filled with crushed ice. Refreshing!

In late summer, when the purple grapes are ripe....try this one for pure enjoyment:

GRAPE JUICE

Wash grapes and boil until skin, pulp and seeds separate. Press through jelly bag and to every pint of juice add one half cup of sugar. Boil for twenty minutes, chill. When ready to serve, pour over crushed ice.

And then there's a grape wine (for the stomach's sake!)

GRAPE WINE

If you want to start with fresh grapes just from the vine....pick a lot! Wash grapes and remove stems. Cook until skin, pulp and seed separate. Prepare the juice as above (strain through jelly bag).

6 quarts of juice
8 cups sugar
1 package yeast

Mix well and pour into a glass or pottery jar. Cover and let stand for about 15 days or until fermentation has ceased. Strain and bottle. Wait two weeks and strain again. Pour in sterilized jars and seal.

TEA PUNCH

3 cups boiling water
10 tea bags (or 10 teaspoons tea
 leaves)
24 whole cloves
1 (3-inch) stick cinnamon, crumbled
2¼ cups fresh lemon juice
1¼ cups fresh orange juice
3 cups sugar
4 quarts cold water
orange and lemon slices

Pour boiling water over tea bags, whole cloves and crumbled stick cinnamon. Cover and simmer for 5 minutes. Strain and cool. Add lemon juice, orange juice and sugar. Stir until sugar is dissolved. Add cold water. Store in refrigerator until ready to use. Then pour into ice filled punch bowl and garnish with lemon and orange slices. Makes 50 cup servings.

LEMONADE

1 cup sugar
1 cup water
rind of 2 lemons
1 cup lemon juice
4 cups ice water

Cut the lemon rind in pieces. Combine sugar, water and rind in saucepan. Stir over low heat until sugar is dissolved. Boil 5 minutes. Cool. Add lemon juice. Remove rind. Pour ice water into mixture. Pour lemonade over ice cubes in a pitcher of glasses. Serves 4 to 6.

You wouldn't call this a "Spring House Cooler".... exactly, but you'd for sure call it a "must" for the holidays.... a recipe popular down through the ages....

MULLED CIDER

¼ cup light brown sugar, firmly packed
4 whole cloves
2 whole allspice, crushed
3 one-inch pieces of stick cinnamon
⅛ teaspoon salt
¼-½ teaspoon grated nutmeg
2 quarts cider

Put all ingredients together in a large saucepan and simmer for ten minutes. Strain and pour into hot mugs. Garnish each with a stick of cinnamon. Serves 10.

General Foods is also responsible for this "cooler".... we've never served it without being asked for the recipe over and over.... so thought it well to share it with you.... it's great for parties any time of the year.

CREAMY COFFEE SODA PUNCH

¼ cup instant Maxwell House Coffee
½ cup sugar
½ cup cold water
1 bottle (1 pt.-12 oz. bottle) Club Soda or Ginger Ale, chilled
1 quart chocolate or coffee ice cream
½ pint whipped cream

Combine coffee, sugar and water in large punch bowl. Stir or beat with a rotary beater until coffee is dissolved. Then stir in soda or ginger ale. Cut quart of ice cream in quarters (or you may prefer to halve it) and put into mixture. Spoon coffee mixture over ice cream until it begins to melt.... place "dollops" of whipped cream on top of punch and serve. This makes 8 to 10 servings. Triple for a group.

This particular recipe was adapted from the original colonial Williamsburg Cookbook and well deserves a place on your "Holiday" entertainment menus.

SYLLABUB

2 cups boiling water
3 Constant Comment tea bags
2 tablespoons sugar
1 cup light sweet wine
1 cup whipped cream
⅛ teaspoon ground mace or allspice

Pour boiling water over tea bags. Steep 5 minutes. Remove tea bags. Add sugar and stir until dissolved. Cool. Pour cool wine into tea. Chill mixture. When ready to serve, pour tea mixture into chilled wine glasses. Spoon whipped cream on top. Sprinkle with a small bit of mace or allspice. You may want to stir before drinking.

Constant Comment Tea is a special blend created by R. C. Begelow. . . . if you haven't tried it, do so! It's just unfortunate it wasn't around for our grandmother's Country Cookin'!

Serve the above in antique goblets or pewter tankards for a real authentic Williamsburg country touch!

This is a beautiful dessert. . . . descended from an Old English recipe and was truly an early "Old South" delight!

"OLD FASHIONED" SYLLABUB

2 cups cream
2 cups milk
½ cup Sherry
½ cup sugar
1/16 teaspoon salt (that's a slight pinch)

Beat the cream, milk, sugar, salt and Sherry together until frothy. Chill thoroughly before serving. Serve in punch cups and sprinkle each serving with nutmeg. Serves 8.

Note: Be sure to whip thoroughly in order to get the light airy substance so important to the real Old Fashioned Syllabub.

Serve this one with your fanciest dinner or just to "cool off" on a hot afternoon. Our source says "It's in a class by itself".

GINGER COCKTAIL

1 cup grapejuice
1 cup unsweetened grapefruit juice
1 cup orange juice
¾ cup lemon juice
½ cup powdered sugar
Ginger Ale
lemon sherbert
chopped crystalized ginger

Combine the juices. Add sugar and stir until dissolved. Chill. When ready to serve, fill small glasses ⅔ full and fill glass with ginger ale. Top with small scoop lemon sherbert and sprinkle with finely chopped ginger.

If you have a small cook in the house let her make this for you on a hot summer's day. It's called. . . .

TEAL'S BANANA COOLER

Use 1 ripe banana for each person to be served. Use 2 cups sweet milk for each person. Blend together in blender until smooth and add: 1 scoop vanilla ice cream for each person. Blend well.
Serve in cold glasses and add a dash of nutmeg on top of each serving. You may also want to put one ice cube in each glass. Delicious and easy to make.
If you do not have a blender, mash bananas until real mushy. Add milk and beat with egg beater. Add ice cream and mix with beater until creamy and smooth.

From Callaway Gardens Restaurants

FROM CALLAWAY GARDENS RESTAURANTS

When you visit Callaway Gardens, one of the most interesting things to do is visit the various dining areas. . . and if you aren't already hungry, after a few minutes studying the menus, or going through the buffet. . . you'll be ready to try any number of the delectable recipes they have for your selection!

If you're a frequent visitor to the Gardens, you already know that in the Plantation Room at the Inn, the buffet table is a most perfect, palatable picture. . . at breakfast, lunch or dinner! A buffet piled high with salads, fruits, fresh vegetables (grown in the Gardens, in season!) . . . meats, chicken and a "plumb sea-worthy" seafood dinner every Friday night! (People drive for miles just to feast on the delicious seafood prepared by the experienced chefs in the Gardens kitchen!).

If you're feeling particularly festive you'll want to make reservations in the Georgia Room where you'll be most pleasantly treated to Elegant dining. . . . served with the utmost care. . . in a relaxing atmosphere.

A trip to the Gardens Restaurant is a treat indeed. . . for here you get a chance to taste some real country cookin'. . . Southern Fried Chicken. . . Barbecue Ribs. . . Apple Pie and many other tasty morsels prepared in the traditional style of the south!

Still another delightful dining area awaits you at the Country Kitchen in the Country Store! After you've browsed through all the international goodies on the shelves. . . "ooo. . ed". . . over the simply beautiful selection of gift items. . . and treated your eyes to shelves filled with all the Callaway Gardens specialities. . . like Blueberry Jam. . . Muscadine Preserves. . . (and dozens more!), then. . . it's time to take a seat on the Country Store Patio overlooking the Mountains below and the Gardens beyond. . . and be served a never-to-be-forgotten Country Ham Sandwich, a scrumptious hamburger with fries or any number of other sandwiches along with favorite beverages.

And now, to give you a chance to taste some of the most popular recipes prepared at the Gardens. . . we invite you to try these recipes at home!

SAM'S FRIED CHICKEN

1 (2½-3 lb.) broiler-fryer chicken
½ cup all-purpose flour
1 teaspoon salt
1 teaspoon paprika
¼ teaspoon pepper
shortening, salad oil or bacon
    drippings

Cut chicken into serving-size pieces and rinse in cold running water, do not dry. Blend dry ingredients in a plastic or brown paper bag. Drop two or three pieces chicken at a time into floured mixture and shake until chicken is coated. In a large heavy skillet heat enough shortening to fill skillet ½-inch deep over high heat until a drop of water sizzles when added to grease. (I find that bacon drippings give the best and tastiest chicken.) Place chicken skin side down in hot fat; put in larger pieces, such as breasts and legs, first. You may need to adjust heat as chicken cooks, lowering to medium high. Turn pieces to brown evenly. Reduce heat to medium-low, cover, and cook about 30 minutes or until tender. Yield: 4-6 servings.

Variation: Add a teaspoon each of dry mustard and thyme to flour mixture, or add a teaspoon of curry powder for a zestier flavor.

CREAM OF PEANUT SOUP

¼ lb. butter
1 stalk celery, chopped
½ medium onion
1 quart chicken broth
½ pint milk
½ quart 18% cream
¼ lb. peanut butter
salt, pepper, paprika to taste
2 tablespoons bread flour

Braise celery and onions in butter. Add flour, chicken stock and bring to a boil. Add milk and cream. Strain. Add peanut butter. Cook slowly for 5 minutes. Season to taste.

QUICHE LORRAINE

4 thin slices bacon
1 medium-size onion, diced
1 oz. mushrooms, chopped
2 teaspoons chopped parsley
1 (9-in) unbaked pie shell
2 ounces Gruyere cheese, cut in-
    to small cubes
3 oz. Old Canadian cheese, cut
    into small cubes
1 pint Half and Half
4 eggs, beaten
dash garlic salt
dash white pepper
dash ground nutmeg

In large skillet saute bacon, onion, mushrooms, and parsley over medium heat; drain off any excess fat and cool. Fill bottom of pie shell with cheeses and sauteed ingredients. Combine cream, beaten eggs, and seasonings and pour into pie shell. Bake in a preheated 400° oven for 10 minutes. Reduce heat to 350° and continue baking for another 30 minutes. Serve warm. Yield: 1 (9 in) quiche, 6 servings.

CORN PUDDING SUPREME

Simply yummy!
3 large eggs, room temperature
2½ cups fresh corn or 2 (10 oz.)
    packages frozen whole ker-
    nal or creamed corn, thawed
½ cup whipping cream
½ cup milk
2 tablespoons all-purpose flour
1 teaspoon salt
2 tablespoons firmly packed dark
    brown sugar
2 tablespoons butter, melted

Beat eggs until light, then add remaining ingredients. Pour into a buttered 1-quart casserole. Bake in a preheated 350° oven for 1 hour. Serve immediately. Yield: 6 servings.

ZUCCHINI SOUFFLE

The zucchini base makes enough for four souffles. Freeze each cup separately. Serve with broiled ham steak and hot biscuits for an unforgettable meal.

3 cups sliced zucchini
  (about 1 lb.)
1 cup water
2 chicken bouillon cubes
1 tablespoon instant minced onion
1 tablespoon dried parsley flakes
1 teaspoon Season-All
2½ tablespoon butter
2 tablespoons all-purpose flour
1 cup beef bouillon
4 egg yolks
¼ teaspoon Tabasco
¼ teaspoon dried green onion
½ teaspoon salt
4 egg whites
¼ teaspoon cream of tartar
⅛ teaspoon paprika

Wash zucchini, slice and place in a large saucepan with water, chicken cubes, instant minced onion, parsley flakes, and Season-All. Bring mixture to a boil over medium-high heat. Cover and cook until zucchini is tender, about 20 minutes. Put through a sieve or puree in a blender; if using blender, put half of mixture in at a time.

Melt butter in a saucepan over low heat. Add and blend in flour stirring constantly with wire whisk. Stir hot bouillon in slowly. Raise heat to medium and cook until sauce is smooth and boiling. This will be very thick. Remove from heat and add egg yolks; beat well. Add one cup zucchini mixture, Tabasco, dried green onion and salt.

Preheat oven to 400°. Beat egg whites until very frothy using high speed of electric mixer. Add cream of tartar and continue beating until the whites are very stiff peaks. Fold in a fourth of the beaten egg whites in souffle mixture to lighten it. Continue folding in egg whites With a spatula, take more than a minute or two. Pour souffle into a 6-cup charlotte mold or a 1½ quart casserole of the bowl type. Sprinkle top of souffle with paprika. Lower heat to 375 and place mold on middle rack of oven. Bake at 375° for 25-30 mintues. A well-cooked souffle will hold 5-10 minutes in a turned-off hot oven. Yield: 6 servings.

Distinctive and mellow.

BANANA NUT BREAD

½ cup butter
½ cup sugar
l large egg, well beaten
1 cup all-bran cereal
1½ cups mashed bananas, 4
   medium-size bananas
2 tablespoons water
1½ cups all-purpose flour,
   measured before sifting
2 teaspoons baking powder
½ teaspoon salt
½ teaspoon soda
1 teaspoon vanilla extract
1 cup chopped pecans or
   walnuts, optional
1 tablespoon flour

Cream butter and sugar until light and fluffy. Add beaten egg and stir in all-bran cereal. Remove white stringy covering before mashing bananas. Combine thoroughly mashed bananas and water; add to creamed mixture. Sift measured flour, baking powder, salt and soda and add to banana mixture gradually. Do not beat, stir gently only until blended. Add vanilla. Fold in chopped nuts that have been coated with 1 tablespoon flour. Spoon batter into a greased loaf pan lined waxed paper. Bake in a preheated 350° oven for 50 minutes or until bread test done. Cool on rack for 10 minutess and remove from pan. This bread freezes well and sliced nicely when frozen. Keep in refrigerator for best taste results. Yield: 1 (8x4x2 inch) loaf.

BREAD PUDDING

1 loaf French bread
1 quart milk
3 eggs
2 cups sugar
2 tablespoons vanilla extract
1 cup seedless raisins
3 tablespoons margarine, melted
1 pint Vanilla Sauce

Soak bread in milk; crush with hands until well mixed. Add eggs, sugar, vanilla, and raisins and stir well. Pour margarine in bottom of a thick, oblong baking pan, add bread mixture, and bake until very firm. Let cool; then cube pudding and put into individual pyrex dessert dishes. Add vanilla sauce. Yield: 8 to 10 servings.

CRABMEAT REMICK WITH HOMEMADE MAYONNAISE

2 egg yolks, cold
⅓ cup lemon juice, strained and
   chilled, divided
2 cups corn or other vegetable
   oil, chilled
1 teaspoon salt
1½ teaspoons Tabasco
1¾ teaspoons dry mustard
1¼ teaspoons paprika
1 teaspoon tarragon vinegar
½ cup chili sauce
5 strips lean bacon
1 pound lump crabmeat

Chill a deep narrow bowl before making mayonnaise. Place egg yolks and 1 teaspoon lemon juice in a bowl and beat at high speed of electric mixer until mixture becomes thicker, then slowly add some oil and continue beating. When mayonnaise begins to thicken, add salt, Tabasco, mustard and paprika. Add a small amount of lemon juice. Gradually add remaining oil. Use lemon juice often to keep mixture from becoming too thick. To every 1¼ cups mayonnaise add given amounts of vinegar and chili sauce; blend well. Cook bacon over medium heat in a skillet until crisp; drain on a paper towel. Carefully pick through crabmeat to remove any tiny pieces of shell. Divide crabmeat into seven piles. Place crabmeat into individual ramekins and top with sauce and bacon strips. Bake in a preheated 400° oven for 10 minutes, change heat to broiler for 1 minute until sauce is bubbling hot. This is delicious with parslied new potatoes or stuffed baked potatoes. Yield: 7 servings.

1½ cups commercial mayon-
   naise
1 teaspoon tarragon vinegar
½ cup chili sauce
1 teaspoon dry mustard
2 tablespoons strained lemon
   juice
1 teaspoon paprika
1 teaspoon Tabasco

Blend all ingredients in a bowl and pour over crabmeat. Top with bacon and bake as directed above.

STEAK TARTARE

2 lbs. ground sirloin or round
　　steak
½ cup finely chopped onion
1 clove garlic, minced
1 teaspoon salt
1 teaspoon freshly ground black
　　pepper
2 tablespoons Worcestershire
　　sauce
¼ cup chopped parsley
⅓ cup cognac
Pumpernickel bread slices,
　　assorted crackers, or melba
　　rounds

Place beef in a large glass or stainless steel bowl; add remaining ingredients. Mix well and refrigerate until serving time. Spread 1 heaping tablespoonful mixture on pumpernickel bread slices, crackers or melba rounds. Yield: about 4 cups, 48 servings.

QUAIL IN RED WINE

12 quail
flour
¾ cup butter
4 cups sliced mushrooms
½ cup butter
2 cups Consomme
2 cups dry red wine
stalk celery
salt and pepper
juice of 8 oranges

Split the quail in half and rub with a cloth soaked in brandy. Dust with flour. Melt ¾ cup butter in flameproof casserole, add quail and brown about 10 minutes. Saute mushrooms in ½ cup of butter and add to casserole. Add consomme, red wine, stalk of celery, salt and pepper. Cover and simmer 20-30 minutes or until quail are tender. Discard celery and add strained orange juice. Serve pipping hot.

Georgia Room

This delicous dish unites breast of chicken with heart of artichoke. Easy to prepare and excellent for company, it may be made a day ahead and reheated. Serve with fluffy rice or noodles and a tossed green salad for a complete meal.

CHICKEN IBERVILLE

6 chicken breasts, skinned
½ teaspoon salt
⅛ teaspoon white pepper
¼ teaspoon paprika
3 tablespoon butter
½ cup chopped celery
1 3-oz. can button mushrooms
   or ½ lb. large fresh
   mushrooms, trimmed,
   washed and dried, and diced
2 cups hot chicken bouillon or
   2 cups hot beef bouillon
3 tablespoons sifted all-purpose
   flour
4 tablespoons sherry
1 14-oz. can artichoke hearts,
   drained and rinsed, cut into
   fourths

Sprinkle breasts with salt, white pepper and paprika and saute in butter over medium heat in a heavy skillet. Remove when lightly golden on both sides. Saute mushrooms in same skillet. Add an additional tablespoon of butter if mushrooms tend to stick. Add hot chicken bouillon and stir in sifted flour. Add sherry, if desired. Place chicken breasts and artichoke hearts in a buttered 2-quart oblong baking dish and cover with mushroom mixture. Bake in a preheated 375° oven for 40 minutes. Yield: 6 servings. Add 1 tablespoon of Hollandaise Sauce on each serving.

At Callaway Gardens there are so many good things served to eat. . . . it's hard to decide what you like best. . . . but one dessert you'll always enjoy is the delicious

RITZ PECAN PIE

⅔ cup egg whites
1 cup sugar
16 Ritz crackers, crumbled
¼ pound chopped pecans
½ teaspoon baking powder

Beat the egg whites. Mix sugar and baking powder. Add to egg whites. Beat until stiff peak. Fold in nuts and cracker crumbs. Bake 45 minutes at 300°. When cooled, top with whipped cream. Garnish with extra cracker crumbs and pecans.

Our thanks to the chef who shared this one!

BARBECUED SPARE RIBS AU SAUCE

1 med. onion, chopped fine
2 tablespoon vinegar
2 tablespoons brown sugar
2 tablespoons lemon juice
1 cup catsup
3 tablespoons Worchestershire
    sauce
1/2 teaspoon mustard
1/2 cup water
1/2 cup celery
1/2 teaspoon chili powder
salt
red pepper

Brown ribs in oven until tender then add sauce and continue to simmer 30-40 minutes until flavor has cooked into ribs.

ICED TEA SUPERB

3 tablespoons tea (choice blend
    of Indian and Ceylon)
1 small bundle of fresh mint
    leaves
3 teacups cold water, brought to
    a boil
3/4 cup sugar
juice of 2 med.-size limes,
    strained

Scald the teapot. (Use a china or earthenware pot; metal spoils the flavor). Place tea and mint leaves in pot and add boiling water. Allow to stand 5 minutes strain tea into a pitcher, never a metal one such as aluminum or tin.) When the tea is slightly cooled, add lime juice and serve over crushed ice. Yield: 4-5 glasses.

170

Gardens Restaurant

Callaway Gardens is known for the beautiful blueberries grown there. . . . and lucky are the patrons who visit during blueberry season! Blue berries over ice cream . . . . blueberry muffins and . . . .

BLUEBERRY PIE

4 cups blueberries
1 cup sugar
4 tablespoons all purpose flour
½ teaspoon pumpkin pie spice
⅛ teaspoon salt
1 tablespoon lemon juice
1 tablespoon butter

Have prepared pastry for a two crust pie. (Your favorite or a mix.) Wash and pick the berries. Remove stems. Combine berries, sugar, flour and spices and salt. Line a 9-inch pie plate with crust. Pour in the fruit mixture. Sprinkle with lemon juice and dot with one tablespoon butter. Cover with top crust. Flute the edges (dampen fingers to do this), sprinkle with sugar and bake in 400° oven for 35-40 minutes. Serve with a scoop of vanilla ice cream . . . . or whipped cream . . . . or . . . . for something different, try a tablespoon of frozen cream cheese (a suggestion from our New England friends!). They take an 8-oz. pkg. of cream cheese, soften it . . . . add ½ cup sugar, 1 teaspoon vanilla, 1 egg and 2 pints of vanilla ice cream. Blend all together and turn into a 9x5x3 loaf pan and freeze (cover top with waxed paper). Cut in squares and serve on your pie!

HAM WITH RED GRAVY

4 slices country-cured ham
½ inch thick
1½ cups boiling water

Soak ham slices in cold water at least 6 hours (it is very salty). Dry on paper toweling. Remove hard black rind. Put slice into ungreased heavy skillet at fairly high heat. Fry each side 5 to 7 minutes to a good brown, but do not burn. Remove slices to platter, pour off all but 3 tablespoons of fat. Put pan back on stove so it is smoking hot. Add boiling water. Let boil up and be sure to scrape all "fry" from the bottom to blend into the gravy. Pour over the ham slices and serve with grits.

Too Good
To Be Left Out!

TOO GOOD TO BE LEFT OUT

Compiling a cookbook is no easy task. . . but a lot of fun! It really doesn't matter how long you work at it. . . you always end up "adding these. . . taking out those". . and then you have a file of wonderful recipes that really should have been included. . . but **that** chapter is finished. . . so what else to do but have an **extra** chapter (or section!) and simply title it just what it is. . . . "Too Good To Be Left Out!"

You'll find some really delicious recipes on the following pages which we found to be just that. . . Too Good To Be Left Out of "Country Cookin' from Callaway Gardens"!

COUNTRY SUPPER PIE

½ cup tomato sauce
½ cup toasted bread crumbs
⅓ cup chopped onion
½ pound ground beef (lean)
¼ cup chopped green pepper
1½ teaspoon salt
⅛ teaspoon oregano
⅛ teaspoon black pepper
Filling:
2 cups cooked rice
1½ cups tomato sauce
1 cup grated Cheddar Cheese
½ teaspoon salt

Combine these ingredients and mix well. Pat meat mixture into bottom and sides of 9-inch pie plate. Pinch 1-inch fluting around edge. Set aside.

Combine rice, tomato sauce, salt and ¼ cup of the cheese. Spoon mixture into the meat crust. Cover with aluminum foil. Bake in 350° oven for 25 minutes. Uncover and sprinkle with remaining cheese. Return to oven and bake uncovered 10-15 minutes longer. Cut into pie shaped pieces. Serves 6.

CHILI CORN BAKE

2 eggs
1 cup sour cream
1 cup cream style corn
1 cup cornbread mix
¼ cup bacon drippings
⅔ cup grated Cheddar Cheese
⅔ cup cottage cheese
1 small can green chilies
1 small can sliced ripe olives

Grease 1½ quart casserole dish with vegetable shortening or butter, as you prefer. Beat eggs. Add corn and sour cream. Mix well. Add bacon drippings. Mix together in a separate dish the cottage cheese and the Cheddar cheese. Put ½ the corn mixture in the casserole. Put half the green chilies on top of the corn mixture. Sprinkle half of the sliced ripe olives over this. Put a layer of half of the Cheddar cheese mixture over this. Repeat the process of corn, chilies, olives and cheese. Mix the cornbread mix according to the package directions. Spread over the top of mixture in casserole. Bake in 425° oven for 25 minutes or until topping is done. It has to be one of the tastiest dishes you've ever eaten.

Here's a bean dish you can whip up in no time! Take five minutes to get it from the freezer and pantry shelf, just a few minutes more to cook and mix and you'll love the results.

LIMA BEAN CASSEROLE

1 (10-oz.) pkg. frozen lima beans
   (small variety)
2 tablespoons chopped pimento
3 tablespoons chopped chives
1 clove garlic
½ pint sour cream
salt and pepper to taste

Cook beans according to package. Do not overcook! Drain beans and place into casserole dish with pimento and chives, mix thoroughly. Add sour cream and mix well with beans. Fold over rather than stirring, which would crush beans. Place the split garlic bud on a toothpick and inbed in beans in the center of dish. Bake in 325° oven for 20 minutes. Remove toothpick and garlic. Stir once and serve piping hot.

From an old cookbook we selected this recipe as one "Too Good to be Left Out".

SAUTEED NEW POTATOES

Take quanity of tiny new potatoes desired and scrub well. Parboil in salted water to cover. Cook for three minutes and then drain well. Heat 2 tablespoons chicken fat (I suppose you save the grease in which you have cooked chicken, this does very well, helps to season). Cook the potatoes in the hot fat until they are tender and golden brown. Drain and pour the fat from the pan. Place potatoes back in pan and add 2 tablespoons butter for each cup of potatoes. Roll the potatoes around in the butter as it melts. Season with a little salt and pepper and sprinkle with finely chopped parsley. SO good!

Don't know who created this particular mixture for celery, but do know you'll want to pass it on to your friends.

STUFFED CELERY

8 oz. package cream cheese
1 teaspoon vinegar
1 tablespoon cream
1 teaspoon curry powder
5 tablespoons chutney
several stalks of firm celery

Cut the celery stalks into short serving pieces and chill in ice water until very crisp. Cream the cheese. Add the vinegar, cream and curry powder. Blend until well blended and smooth. Add the chutney which you have chopped until fine. Store in refrigerator until right consistency to fill celery. When ready to serve, dry the celery pieces and pile up with the filling.

Note: Filling will be quite "gooey" when first mixed but will harden as it chills in the refrigerator.

GARDEN EGG SALAD

½ cup mayonnaise or salad
    dressing
⅓ cup sweet pickle relish
½ teaspoon celery salt
½ teaspoon instant minced onion
8 hard-cooked eggs, chopped
1 package frozen peas (10 oz.)
¼ cup chopped celery
Lettuce leaves, optional

In medium bowl, stir together mayonnaise, relish, celery salt and onion until blended. Toss with eggs, peas and celery until combined. Cover and chill to blend flavors. Serve on lettuce leaves, if desired. Makes 4 main dish or 8 salad servings.

Try this one with your shrimp, a quick and easy cocktail sauce.

BOILED SHRIMP SAUCE

Cook your shrimp, peel and chill.
¾ cup hot tomato catsup
¼ cup horseradish
1 tablespoon Worcestershire sauce
1 teaspoon lime (or lemon) juice

Mix all ingredients. Chill and serve with the chilled shrimp and hot toasted buttered crackers.

Too Good To Be Left Out

Simply delicious barbecue sauce to use over ribs, ham or chicken.

ZESTY BARBECUE SAUCE

1 cup canned tomatoes
1 cup bouillon
1 cup wine
¼ cup lemon juice
⅓ cup Worcestershire sauce
½ cup olive oil
¼ teaspoon Tabasco sauce
1 bottle chili sauce
½ cup finely chopped celery
1 cup finely chopped onion
½ teaspoon basil
½ teaspoon oregano
1 teaspoon chili powder
¼ cup sugar
1 teaspoon salt
1 teaspoon coarsely ground black
   pepper
½ teaspoon crushed red peppers
1 bay leaf

Combine all ingredients and bring to a boil. Lower heat and simmer for 1 hour. Remove bay leaf. This may be refrigerated until needed.

Want a quick, fool proof recipe for Hollandaise? Try this one.

HOLLANDAISE SAUCE

3 egg yolks
2 tablespoons lemon juice
⅓ teaspoon grated lemon peel
½ teaspoon prepared mustard
⅛ teaspoon cayenne pepper
½ cup butter

Put egg yolks, lemon juice, lemon peel, mustard and cayenne in blender. Blend until all ingredients are mixed well. Heat butter in saucepan till melted and hot. While blender is slowly running pour in about ⅓ of the hot butter, pouring in a thin stream. Then turn blender to high speed and add remaining hot butter. Blend until smooth and thickened. Best when served immediately. Great over hot vegetables.

178

Try this on your fresh cooked green beans.

MUSTARD SAUCE

¼ cup prepared mustard (prefer French style)
2 tablespoons vinegar
½ teaspoon salt
¼ cup olive oil or salad oil
⅛ teaspoon Tabasco sauce

Combine all ingredients and mix thoroughly. Chill well before serving on your vegetables, particularly green beans.

For your fruit salads, try this:

SUNKIST HONEY DRESSING

⅓ cup mayonnaise
¼ cup honey
1 tablespoon fresh grated orange peel
3 tablespoons fresh squeezed orange juice
1 tablespoon fresh squeezed lemon juice
½ teaspoon paprika

Combine all ingredients, blend well. Serve over any fresh fruit. Particularly good over grapefruit, orange and pineapple and/or banana sections.

This one was just too good to be left out too, and a grand sauce for ham or turkey.

CRANBERRY CHUTNEY SAUCE

1 can jellied cranberry sauce
½ cup sugar
½ cup vinegar
2 teaspoons salt
1 tablespoon curry powder
½ teaspoon ginger
1 tablespoon Worcestershire sauce
1 tablespoon molasses
1 teaspoon Tabasco

Crumble jellied cranberry sauce in saucepan. Add remaining ingredients. Beat with a rotary beater. Bring to a boil over moderate heat. Reduce heat and simmer for 5-8 minutes. Blend with rotary beater until smooth.

You may want to substitute whole cranberry sauce, mix as with jellied, but do not mash the cranberries. Good as a condiment.

Here's a bit of spice and luscious goodness from the Sunkist Kitchens which will go good with meats or vegetables. Also makes a good "neighborly gift" from your kitchen. . . .

SPICY CITRUS TOMATO CONSERVE

3 medium Sunkist oranges, unpeeled
8-9 large, firm, ripe tomatoes (the kind which grows in Mr. Cason's Garden), you need enough to make 8 cups
7 cups sugar
1/3 cup fresh squeezed lemon juice
1 tablespoon whole cloves
2 sticks cinnamon
1 cup golden or dark raisins

Cut a thin slice from each end of the oranges and discard. Cut fruit in half, lenghtwise. Remove white center core and any seeds. Place cut side down on cutting board and cut into thinest slices possible. Then cut slices in half. Combine with tomatoes (which have been peeled, cored and sliced), sugar and lemon juice. Place in a six quart saucepot. Add spices which you have tied loosely in a cheesecloth square. Bring to a boil, reduce heat and gently boil uncovered for one hour. Stir frequently to avoid sticking. Remove spice bag and add raisins. Reduce heat slightly and slowly simmer about 20 minutes longer. Mixture will be reduced and clear, but syrup will not be extra thick. Pour into hot sterilized jars and seal.

So good!

BAKED CHEESE CUSTARD WITH TOAST

6 slices bacon
1½ cups grated Swiss cheese
1½ cups grated parmesan cheese
2 cups heavy cream
3 eggs, well beaten
1 teaspoon salt
½ teaspoon dried basil
dash pepper and paprika
toasted bread

Start oven at moderate (350ºF). Butter 1½ quart baking dish. Fry bacon until crisp; drain and crumble. Combine bacon, cheese, cream, eggs and seasonings. Pour into baking dish. Place dish in shallow pan of warm water. Bake in preheated moderate oven about 35 minutes or longer, until set. It should be the consistency of thick custard, or slightly firmer. Serve warm, from baking dish onto toasted bread. Makes 6 servings.

CRANBERRY-SHERRY JELLY

2 cups White wine
4 cups raw cranberries
2 cups sugar
1 cup Sherry
1 tablespoon lemon juice
pinch of salt
2 envelopes gelatin
1/4 cup cold water

Bring the White wine to a boil and add the 4 cups raw cranberries and cook over low heat for 30 minutes. Pour the mixture through a strainer lined with cheesecloth and discard the cranberry pulp. Combine the cranberry juice with 2 cups sugar, the Sherry, the lemon juice and salt. Cook over medium heat for about 5 minutes. Remove from heat and stir in the gelatin which has been softened in the cold water. Let the mixture cool and pour into one large mold or into jelly glasses. Chill until firm. If you are using as a large mold for a party. . . . unmold on a chilled plate. . . garnish with parsley or holly leaves around bottom of mold. If using as individual molds from jelly glasses (or smaller containers for individual servings), unmold on chilled salad plate and garnish with same greenery and a small "dollop" of whipped cream on top of each serving.

BAKED CUSTARD

2 large eggs or 4 egg yolks
1/3 cup sugar
1/4 teaspoon salt
2 cups milk
nutmeg for flavoring
vanilla may be added also

Beat the eggs or yolks slightly until mixed. Add the sugar and salt and mix. Scald the milk, and carefully add to the egg mixture. Add flavoring. Strain into six custard cups and set in a pan into which, pour 1 inch of hot water. Bake 30-35 minutes at 350°F. or until a silver knife inserted into the custard comes out clean. Immediately remove the cups from the hot water. Serve hot or cold. Serves 6.

A country cookbook would not be complete without the recipe for one of the South's favorite breads. . . that delightful "immigrant from 18th century Britian". . . .

SALLY LUNN

4 cups enriched self-rising flour
1 package yeast
1 cup milk
¾ cup butter
¼ cup sugar
4 eggs

Stir together the yeast and 2 cups of the flour. Heat the milk, butter and sugar over low heat until warm, stirring to blend. Add liquid ingredients to flour-yeast mixture and beat until smooth. Blend in eggs. Add 1 cup flour and beat for 1 minutes on medium speed (if using mixture, about 200 strokes by hand). Stir in 1 cup flour and pour into large well greased bowl. Cover and let rise in warm place until doubled (about 1½ hours). Stir down. Pour into well greased 4 quart mold and let rise until doubled (40-45 minutes). Bake in preheated oven, 375°, for 45 minutes or until done. Cool and remove from mold and enjoy!

Pecans, one of the "Five p's" of Georgia (that's poultry, peaches, peanuts, pimentos and pecans, if you've forgotten). Georgia grows some of the finest, Stuarts being among the very best. Try some with this recipe for:

SPICED PECANS

1 pound pecans
¼ pound butter
1 teaspoon grated nutmeg
¼ cup sugar
⅛ teaspoon salt

Preheat oven to 325°. Place pecans in shallow pan or dish. Roast for 20 minutes, stirring frequently, turning halves over and over. Melt butter in saucepan with sugar and nutmeg. Pour over pecans and put back in oven for a few minutes. Keep stirring and turning until pecans have absorbed most of the butter mixture. Pour out on paper towels to dry. Store in airtight containers.

PEARS IN WINE

1 cup sugar
1 cup water
4 Barlett or 12 Seckel pears
5 whole cloves
1 cup burgundy

Cook sugar with water until syrupy, stirring frequently until sugar is all dissolved. Peel pears, but leave whole. . preferably with stems on. . add wine and cloves. Simmer gently until pears are tender, 20-25 minutes. Let chill in syrup.

If served as a dessert and you're not afraid of the calories. . . . add a spoonful of whipped cream on top of each pear. . . . serve in your favorite glass stemware.

A drop of red food coloring (or green) to the syrup before adding pears gives another "bit of eye appeal."

This recipe for a most favorite dessert is one I know you will enjoy. It's called:

HEAVENLY HASH

1 (8¾-oz) can pineapple chunks
1 cup Angel Flake coconut
1 cup miniature marshmallows
⅓ cup maraschino cherries, chopped
⅓ cup pecans, chopped
1 carton (4½-oz) Cool Whip, or you may use fresh whipped cream

Drain the pineapple. Toss with coconut, marshmallows, cherries and pecans. Fold in Cool Whip or whipped cream and chill thoroughly before serving. Serves 6. At the holiday season, serve in your prettiest crystal dessert dishes and top with red cherry and mint leaves.

A carry over from the British to America's Countryside. That dessert of desserts:

TRIFLE

4 eggs
½ cup sugar
1 cup milk
1 cup cream
½ vanilla bean (or ½ teaspoon vanilla)
medium size jelly roll
Sherry or Maderia wine

Beat egg yolks until light and stir in ½ cup sugar. Gradually add the milk and cream which you have scalded with the vanilla bean. Cook the mixture over hot water, stirring constantly until it coats the spoon. Strain and cool, stirring occasionally.

Line the bottom and sides of a large glass bowl with half inch slices of the jelly roll. Moisten with Sherry or Maderia wine. Fill the bowl with the cooled custard. Top with dollops of whipped cream.

Angel Food Cake may be used instead of the jelly roll and if you use this type cake, when you place it in the bowl in thick slices, top with spoons of raspberry jam before adding the custard. Really delicious!

SOME DELICIOUS MORSELS YOU DON'T WANT TO MISS
Honey dew balls soaked in Creme de Menthe
Canteloupe balls soaked in orange juice, lemon juice and rum.

Pile a salad plate high with slices of canteloupe, apple, pineapple and Callaway Gardens blueberries. Top with a combination of French dressing, orange juice and shredded apple (not too country, but not too "gourmetish" either).

Boiled shrimp, ice cold, served with a sauce made of olive oil, wine, vinegar, Digon mustard, scallions, celery, horseradish, parsley and your favorite seasonings. That's really "up-country"!

Index

A

B

C

M

N

O

P

Q

R